The Justice Gap

Whatever happened to legal aid?

Steve Hynes is the director of LAG. Until joining LAG in 2007 he was the director of the Law Centres Federation.

Jon Robins is the communications and campaigns director at LAG. He is also a freelance journalist and author.

The Legal Action Group (LAG) is a national, independent charity which campaigns for equal access to justice for all members of society.

Legal Action Group:
- provides support to the practice of lawyers and advisers
- inspires developments in that practice
- campaigns for improvements in the law and the administration of justice
- stimulates debate on how services should be delivered.

Founded in 1971, LAG seeks to improve law and practice, the administration of justice and legal services by publishing a monthly journal, *Legal Action*, and a range of law books, providing professional development courses and promoting policy debate.

Further information can be obtained by contacting the Legal Action Group, 242 Pentonville Road, London, N1 9UN, UK, telephone (+44) 0207 833 2931, fax (+44) 0207 837 6094.

The Justice Gap

Whatever happened to legal aid?

Steve Hynes and Jon Robins

LAG Legal Action Group
2009

This edition published in Great Britain 2009
by LAG Education and Service Trust Limited
242 Pentonville Road, London N1 9UN
www.lag.org.uk

British Library Cataloguing in Publication Data
a CIP catalogue record for this book is available from the British Library.

Crown copyright material is produced with the permission of the
Controller of HMSO and the Queen's Printer for Scotland.

ISBN 978 1 903307 63 2

 This book has been produced using Forest Stewardship
Council (FSC) certified paper. The wood used to produce FSC
certified products with a 'Mixed Sources' label comes from
FSC certified well-managed forests, controlled sources and/or
recycled material.

Typeset by Regent Typesetting, London
Printed in Great Britain by Hobbs the Printers, Totton, Hampshire

Foreword

by Baroness Helena Kennedy QC

Legal aid is an essential component of our welfare system. If there was no system of legal aid intolerable inequalities would become the norm in our society. The kind of miscarriages of justice that shattered public confidence in the justice system throughout the 1980s and 1970s would be commonplace and ordinary people would have no redress against unscrupulous landlords and dodgy bosses.

The Legal Action Group's *The Justice Gap* is a timely publication. It marks the 60th anniversary of the Legal Aid and Advice Act and represents the first major critique of the present Government's lamentable record on legal aid. The book provides a history of access to justice and the legal aid system as well as a commentary on New Labour's attempts to reform the system. The book details the shortcomings of the present system and makes recommendations for improvements.

Crucially, *The Justice Gap* attempts to reassert the principles on which the legal aid system was founded. The role of publicly-funded law in securing access to justice urgently needs to be recognised and, without a clear understanding of those principles that underpin the scheme, legal aid is in danger of withering away as it slips further down the list of government priorities.

The majority of the population will never be faced with a criminal charge but many people will face a civil legal problem in their lives. Unfortunately, it is not until they are confronted with a legal problem that they appreciate the importance of legal aid and the inadequacy in the scope and accessibility of such services. The current government has used this public indifference to downgrade the importance of what was originally intended to be the legal services pillar of the welfare state.

Most shamefully they have taken to denigrating the many dedicated lawyers and advisers who provide help to society's most needy. Over the years they have been known by different names – poor man's lawyers, radical lawyers, alternative lawyers, or civil liberties lawyers. They work in offices and chambers up and down the country putting in long hours and for far less money than the sums bandied around in the press. Their role in our society delivering access to justice needs to be recognised.

This book makes clear that the so called reforms to legal aid have served only to significantly weaken it. The withdrawal of public funding from personal injury claims, for example, has contributed to the exploitation of the most vulnerable accident victims at the hands of the claims farming industry. In an increasingly desperate move to control costs the government seems set to introduce competitive tendering for criminal and civil cases, but has latterly admitted that they do not expect to save any money from this if it goes ahead. The 'phoney market' approach to reform will lead to legal aid becoming even more inaccessible as firms and agencies will be forced out by larger firms driven by the profit motive. (Many have already abandoned the system in response to falling pay rates and increasing bureaucracy.)

At the beginning of 2009 the economic outlook is worse than it has been for twenty years and there will be increasing pressure on legal aid. Ordinary people will face problems caused by unemployment and rising crime rates. The government must respond to the challenge by ensuring that people have access to legal advice and representation to prevent miscarriages of justice and deliver social justice. To do this, they will have to confront the reality of the limitations of the system they have created such as the growth in criminal legal aid expenditure eating into a fixed civil legal aid budget. This book is an important contribution to an essential debate that we need to have about how to best create a legal aid system fit for the 21st century.

April 2009

Acknowledgements

We would like to thank the many people who helped and agreed to be interviewed for the book. We would also like to express our gratitude to Carl Lygo, principal of the Law School, and Kara E Irwin director of the Pro Bono Centre at the BPP for sponsoring the book.

Special thanks to Monique Barns, Legal Action Group publisher.

Chapter 1: Thanks to the volunteers who helped with research, namely Ben Emerson, Katie Tween, Giuseppina Sanna and Federica Velardo.

Chapter 7: We are grateful to Professor John Peysner, professor of law at Lincoln Law School, and David Marshall, managing partner of Anthony Gold solicitors for reading this chapter.

Chapter 8: Thanks to Professor Ed Cape, director of Centre for Legal Research at Bristol Law School, who read this chapter. Thanks also to Anthony Edwards, senior partner at TV Edwards; Andrew Keogh, vice chairman of the Criminal Law Solicitors Association and partner at Keoghs; and Rodney Warren, director of the Criminal Law Solicitors Association for their input.

The press team at the Legal Services Commission has been extremely helpful in answering our many inquiries. Thanks also to Sir Michael Bichard, the former chair of the LSC; Carolyn Regan, chief executive of the LSC; Crispin Passmore, strategy director; Derek Hill, policy director; Richard Collins, former executive director of policy; and all at the LSC who gave up time to be interviewed. We are grateful also to Steve Orchard, former chief executive of the Legal Aid Board and Legal Services Commission and Lord Falconer of Thoroton for their time.

We would also like to mention Sir Geoffrey Bindman, Helena Kennedy QC, Roger Smith, director of JUSTICE and former director of LAG, Richard Miller, legal aid manager at the Law Society. Their support was very much appreciated.

Contents

x

Introduction: the justice gap

At the time of writing in early 2009, the country is in the grip of a growing economic crisis. The number of people losing their jobs is on the sharpest incline since the recession of the early 1990s, and the number of homes being repossessed is rocketing, with some 120 people losing their homes each day. At this time, perhaps more than any other period in the last decade, people of all means need access to good quality legal advice.

It is 60 years since our system of legal aid was first conceived as part of the welfare state; however, we are now at an impasse. Fewer than one in three of us are eligible for help under a scheme that has slowly but steadily been eroded. Campaigners have spoken out increasingly vociferously about legal aid 'desertification' where tracts of England and Wales are left with little or no access to free legal advice. Practitioners complain bitterly about the demoralising cumulative impact of years of continuous reform, pay freezes, or begrudging rises in rates that have long fallen behind inflation. There is compelling evidence of private practice law firms leaving publicly-funded law.

It is inaccurate to suggest that legal aid has entered some new period of crisis. However, that 'crisis', as a result of a long-term absence of vision on the part of those that run legal aid together with an alienated supplier base, has became a way of life for the sector.

This book is the Legal Action Group's (LAG's) contribution to a debate about the future of legal aid at a time when that future – certainly, that of the civil scheme – seems far from certain. *The Justice Gap* attempts to identify the principles that LAG believes should underpin a modern legal aid system. The book also seeks to make a case for its place among the other vital public services and to look forward and identify proposals for improving access to justice. Legal aid was recently described as the 'most friendless wing of the welfare state'.[1] Perhaps above all, the book seeks to explain why an unfairly under-valued, embattled but essential public service like legal aid still matters and why that service should be supported by public and politicians alike.

So, let's start with a question: why does the concept of equal 'access to justice' matter today? As good a place as any to begin to answer that question is Dover county court one Wednesday morning in mid-April 2008 when research for *The Justice Gap* began. Courts like this up and down the country occupy the frontline of the so-called credit crunch. It was repossessions day and the presiding judge District Judge Parnell had 35 cases listed. According to the court listings, his caseload included six mortgage possession cases where lenders were taking legal action to reclaim properties and seven 'suspended' possession cases where, if the homeowner defaulted one more time, lenders could go for immediate eviction.

On the day LAG visited the court, people's homes were literally on the line. 'People often arrive traumatised,' Jacqui O'Carroll told *Legal Action*. Anxious homeowners struck deals with the mortgage company 'agents' – usually local solicitors, often trainees, instructed to act on the behalf of the company – either to pay back arrears in stages or to give up their home. Most people turned up at the court, having received a summons, without any independent advice and often resigned to losing their home.

'Homeowners arrive unsure of what's going on, totally ill-informed, and prepared to lose everything because they think there's no alternative,' said O'Carroll, manager of the legal services unit at Shepway Citizens Advice Bureau who also ran the court advice desk. 'The pressure is huge especially from the less scrupulous providers who will insist they'll get possession and even tell homeowners not to bother to turn up.'

The reality is that in 21st century Britain you can lose the roof over your head – often unnecessarily – through a legal process, in ignorance of the law, and after having been misled about any rights you might have, without having access to publicly-funded legal advice. As O'Carroll explained to those in the court waiting room, borrowers are entitled to repay debts over the remaining period of the mortgage no matter what the lenders tell them (as laid down in the 1995 landmark ruling *Cheltenham & Gloucester Building Society v Norgan*[2]).

Few, if any, homeowners who came into Dover county court that day took legal advice. They did not see the need to. 'Does anybody need help?' O'Carroll asked when no one knocked on the door of her office. Occasionally she took a more proactive approach, interjecting between homeowners and mortgage company reps as they bashed out deals ('Would you like to have a quick chat with me before you agree to anything?'). It quickly became apparent that homeowners were routinely committing themselves to hopelessly unrealistic repayment schemes that they could not afford for fear of losing their homes, or even voluntarily agreeing to give them up.

So where does legal aid fit into this dismal picture? For a start, many homeowners will by definition be barred from the legal aid scheme. Public funding is only available to people who have less than £100,000 equity in their home (their disposable income has to be less than £649 per month). The advice available from O'Carroll, however, was not subject to any means test, though its provision is arbitrary. At the time of LAG's visit, the Legal Services Commission (LSC), which runs the legal aid scheme, funded 94 advice services out of 230 county courts. Within three months of the *Legal Action* report, the LSC made funding available for another 20 schemes.

LAG argues that a critical test for our legal aid system is not just that homeowners fearful of losing their homes should receive proper independent advice about their legal rights. It is also crucial that people understand that they have that right, that there is an adequately funded network of advisers well-placed to provide it, and that those services are clearly signposted. The legal aid system in 2008 falls well short of that.

Without a coherent set of principles, our modern system of legal aid flounders and that has been a considerable part of the story of the recent period. The book starts with a statement of foundation principles that LAG believes should underpin a legal system for the 21st century.

(1) Access to justice is the constitutional right of each citizen

Legal aid was meant to ensure this. The Rushcliffe report, which was the basis on which the modern legal aid system was founded, stated that legal aid should be available in those types of cases in which lawyers normally represented private individual clients. Legal aid should not be limited to those people 'normally classed as poor, but should include those of 'small or moderate means'. The legal aid system never fully realised these ideals. Currently civil legal aid is in danger of becoming a sink service for a minority of the population.

(2) The right to access justice applies equally to civil and criminal law

Civil legal aid, particularly social welfare law, has always been the poor relation in the system. The civil legal aid budget urgently needs to be separated from the growing criminal budget.

(3) The interests of the citizen should determine policy on access to justice issues, not those of the providers of services

Up until 1988 the Law Society administered legal aid. It ran the system largely in the interests of lawyers as opposed to the public. Legal aid policy is still mainly determined by interest groups and not the users of legally aided advice services. The public is not consulted over the type of system they want.

(4) The constitutional right to be regarded as innocent until proved guilty should be respected as a cardinal principle of criminal law

Legal aid was first established at the beginning of the last century for criminal cases as it was increasingly recognised legal representation was essential to guarantee a fair trial. Criminal legal aid is under pressure due to the numerous changes in the law and the administration of justice, but the government fails to recognise this. Equally the inadequacy of some publicly funded services is undermining the protection of defendants' rights under legislation such as the Police and Criminal Evidence Act 1984 and the Human Rights Act 1998.

(5) Promoting access to justice requires policies across a range of areas including law reform, education and legal services

The legal aid system has become too focused on funding individual cases. It has neglected its role in wider legal education and the more creative use of the law to tackle legal problems systematically.

(6) Proposals for reform must take account of the realistic levels of resources but these should not be seen as defining policy

The modern legal aid system has been designed on the basis of the legal services that can be bought within the current budget of £2 billion rather than an understanding of who should qualify under the scheme and to what assistance they should be entitled.

1   *Guardian* 11 October 2006 (Jonathan Freedland).
2   [1996] 1 WLR 343.

CHAPTER 1

Early days: poor man's law

From ancient times to the modern day, it has been recognised that a person's legal rights are often only enforceable if he or she has the services of a lawyer. The principle of free access to justice was enshrined in the Magna Carta in 1215. In the past those unfortunate enough not to be able to afford a lawyer had to rely on the variable public-spiritedness of lawyers for unpaid advice. It was not until the latter half of the last century that the state stepped in to provide for publicly-funded legal services for the majority of the population who could not afford to pay for them. It was the Attlee government that introduced a system of legal aid as an essential part of our welfare state in 1949. This chapter relates to the history of such services and their influence in the development of the state-funded service in the UK.

In the 4th century AD under Emperor Valentinian the office of defensor was introduced to 'defend the towns, the churches, and the humiliors (lower classes) against the powerful and the public functionaries' for those parts of Europe still controlled by the Roman Empire (not including Britain).[1] In the medieval period in Europe the office of advocatus pauperum deputatus et stipendiatus, an official under canon law, was responsible for representing the poor in ecclesiastical courts. This practice spread to the civil courts in parts of France and Italy. Under a statute introduced by Henry VII in 1495 judges were obliged to assign counsel to the poor. The procedure was called in forma pauperis and the poor were also expressly exempt from paying a fee for writs. The statute decreed: 'Every poor person ... shall have ... writ or writs ... according to the nature of their causes, therefore paying nothing to your Highness for the seals of the same, nor to any person for the writing of the same.'[2]

Henry's statute built on the principle of free access to justice enshrined in the Magna Carta in 1215 which contained King John's declaration: 'We will sell to no man, we will not deny or defer to any man either Justice or Right.' In an early example of the state penalising people believed to be the undeserving poor, an unsuccessful litigant could be flogged if he received aid and lost his case.

Christian charity together with secular notions of nobility and chivalry were the main motivations behind these early examples of legal aid.[3] They were reliant on lawyers working for no fee or 'pro bono publico'. The phrase (literally, 'in the public good') is still used to describe the good works lawyers do for no payment, despite the fact that many lawyers believe it would do their public image some good to drop the Latin in the 21st century. A point made by a former Lord Chief Justice, Lord Woolf in 2002: 'I think one reason why pro bono is not playing its part in the provision of legal services as it should, is because of the very words pro bono.'

John Cooke, a radical lawyer and devout Christian, advocated in his book *The Poor Man's Case*, published in 1648, that barristers should be required to donate 10 per cent of their time to working pro bono. Cooke also argued that doctors should treat the poor for no charge. His ideas were inspired by religious conviction and conceived at a time when the concept of equality before the law was taking root. Cooke led the prosecution of Charles I in 1649, the first trial of a head of state for war crimes.[4] His idea of an organised legal aid system in which lawyers provided pro bono services as part of their professional duty was not taken up by parliament in his time. It can be seen as a precursor to the development of legal services to the poor in the late 19th and 20th centuries.

Criminal legal aid: dock briefs

In the first half of the 20th century a partial legal aid system evolved in the criminal courts. Criminal legal aid was introduced for representation of defendants in the higher criminal courts under the Poor Prisoners' Defence Act 1903, if they were deemed to have a defence. The Criminal Appeal Act 1907 ensured legal aid was available in all murder appeals and in some other criminal appeals.

Prior to 1903, prisoners who could not afford a lawyer had to rely on 'dock briefs'. This pro bono system survived up to the establishment of the post-war legal aid scheme. Any wigged and gowned barrister in court could be required to defend an unrepresented prisoner. Unsurprisingly, it was not a popular professional duty amongst the ranks of the Bar. One news report in 1944 refers to the 'general scuttle' of counsel to leave court when a prisoner asked for representation. Often only junior counsel, keen to gain experience and to build a reputation, would be available. One convicted prisoner, the dubious beneficiary of the dock brief system, on being asked if he had anything to say before sentence was passed, complained: 'Nothing, my Lord, except to plead the youth and inexperience of my counsel.'

In 1930 a new criminal legal aid act extended the 1907 scheme to the police courts or magistrates' courts, as they are now known (also advance disclosure of defence was no longer made compulsory). Legal aid was paid from local funds. Any person who was committed to trial for an indictable offence could apply for a defence certificate if he or she did not have the means to pay for legal representation.

Practice on the ground, though, differed widely and was more limited than the generous wording of the statute promised. While the scheme covered all criminal courts, as can be seen by the continuing practice of 'dock briefs', it was not a comprehensive one. The norm for prisoners was not to be represented, especially in the lower courts. In 1938 the police courts, which dealt with the majority of offences, sent 19,079 people to prison. Of that number, only 327 had benefited from representation paid through legal aid certificates.[5]

Civil legal aid: poor man's lawyers

As for civil legal aid in the first half of the 20th century, the majority of the population had no option but to rely on pro bono services for advice and representation. The Poor Man's Lawyer service, which developed in the late 19th century, was a system of organised pro bono help which provided the impetus for social reformers to demand that the state legislate to provide legal aid services to the poor. The service grew out of the settlement movement which was inspired by the work of Samuel Barnett, a clergyman working in the impoverished east end of London. In the 1880s Barnett formulated a radical proposal to bridge, practically and ideologically, the gap between rich and poor by building a boarding house for privileged university graduates in one of the most deprived parts of the east end of London. Modelled on the colleges of Oxford with 'sets' of rooms for the students, library, lecture theatre and various function rooms, Toynbee Hall opened in 1884 on Commercial Street near Aldgate. Barnett wanted to create a community that transcended class barriers, with the graduates providing hands-on educational, social and recreational services to the poor in a spirit of practical neighbourliness. The movement also aimed 'to inquire into the conditions of the poor' and 'to consider and advance plans calculated to promote their welfare'.[6]

This social activism dimension to the settlement movement was led by Frank Tillyard, called to the Bar in 1890, who had founded the first Poor Man's Lawyer service at the Mansfield House settlement. Toynbee Hall and other settlements quickly followed in its wake. Within a few years of Tillyard's pioneering work, the Poor Man's Lawyer was a firmly established charitable service and it was 'common practice for county court judges and police court magistrates to send people who could not afford a lawyer to Poor Man's Lawyer meetings for legal advice'.[7]

By the start of the Second World War, the numbers of such services had increased to 55 in London and 70 in the provinces. Disputes between landlord and tenant, accident cases involving workers' compensation and matrimonial cases involving maintenance and separation were the most common cases dealt with by the services. It was rare though for more than advice to be given due to lack of resources. Frequently only ten minutes could be spared for clients. Obvious weaknesses were the absence of co-operation between the various providers, which were largely dependent on the good will of volunteer lawyers, and a lack of unified system of funding. This led to a call by the settlement movement in 1902 for state funding for a legal aid system that deserving applicants could access by passing a merits test before a public committee. Toynbee Hall set up its own very limited fund to take cases to court and in 1905 it took 23 cases, the most the scheme ever dealt with. The movement felt a 'growing sense of inadequacy' to cope with the demands made upon it.[8]

The 'Poor Man's Lawyer' became a generic term to describe free legal services for the poor and not necessarily associated with the settlement movement. Political parties might organise a service and those provided by local law societies, under what were called the Poor Persons Rules, were often referred to as Poor Man's Lawyer services. For example, the Manchester scheme was run by the local law society and appears to have been the largest service outside London, co-ordinating the work of around 70 firms. At its peak in 1939, these firms advised in 4,290 cases.[9] Coverage was erratic. Towns such as Cardiff and Coventry had no schemes and some towns would deal with far fewer cases than the better served areas like Manchester. For example, the Newcastle scheme dealt with only 198 cases in 1938.

For over 50 years, despite inadequate geographical coverage and limited resources, the Poor Man's Lawyer services remained the only source of legal advice for many people. By the beginning of the 20th century it was becoming apparent that these services could not meet the demand for legal advice. FCG Gurney-Champion, one of the founders of the movement, recognised the limitations of charity in providing access to justice, saying it made the rule of law 'an anaemic attenuated make-believe which we flourish in the eyes of the poor as "justice"'.

The extent of the movement's influence on the eventual establishment of the legal aid system is difficult to assess. But its legacy is easy to spot in the not-for-profit sector, for example in the work of the Mary Ward Legal Centre, as well as an inspiration in the creation of the law centre movement in the early 1970s. As vital as these early initiatives were, it should be acknowledged that their help went only so far and few cases were progressed beyond initial advice, stopping short of representation in the courts.

Poor Persons Rules

Medieval in origin, the in forma pauperis procedure still survived at the beginning of 20th century in much the same form – that is, voluntary help from lawyers on an ad hoc basis. However it was little used due to a stringent means test and the strong social stigma attached to characterising oneself as 'a pauper' necessary to access the scheme.[10] In 1909 only 66 divorce petitions were filed using the procedure.

It was the rising demand for divorce which led to further clamour for the reform of the legal aid available to the poor. Some 50 years after judicial divorce was introduced in 1857 it remained only available in the High Court in London and was prohibitively expensive, costing on average £45 per case (more if witnesses had to be brought from outside London). This was at a time when the average manual wage was £50 per year, and even to get help under the pauperis procedure, a sum of £10 had to be found for solicitors' out-of-pocket expenses.

The pauperis procedural rules were revised by the High Court Rule Committee and renamed the Poor Persons Procedure. When the updated rules were introduced in 1914 a department was created in the Royal Courts of Justice on the Strand in central London to administer the scheme, sift claims and allocate the cases to the volunteer solicitors who staffed the scheme. A combination of social change and the upheaval caused by the First World War led to an even greater demand for divorces. Many people did not want to live with the social stigma of 'living in sin' or illegitimate children. Officials were taken aback by the numbers of applications for help under the revised scheme; in the first week alone of the rules being publicised over 1,000 applications were received.[11] The previous year had seen only 577 divorce decrees in total.[12]

Increased demand and too few solicitors willing to undertake pro bono work led to the government deciding to form a committee headed by a judge, Mr Justice Lawrence, to report on the demand for and availability of legal services to the poor. This was the first in a long line of committees or reviews established by successive governments to examine legal aid.

Lawrence reported in 1919 and concluded that the Poor Persons Rules had generally worked well for non-matrimonial cases, but that they failed people seeking help with divorce proceedings. Out of 2,215 applications in 1918, only half were granted petitions and of these less than half went to trial. The main reason for that was the £10 out-of-pocket expense for the solicitors to proceed with cases.[13] Perversely, Lawrence did not seek to make the system more accessible by reducing the cost. Instead the final recommendations of the committee focused on reducing demand for the service by recommending a more stringent means test and trying to prevent unscrupulous solicitors profiting from the scheme.

Despite the recommendations being implemented, the new scheme was in crisis by December 1920 due to the demand for divorce from people who had no other way to pay. Still not enough solicitors were willing to provide the service and this prompted a second committee to be set up, again chaired by Lawrence.

Reporting in February 1925 the second Lawrence committee confirmed that the system was failing mainly due to the unwillingness of solicitors to undertake the work. It was sympathetic to solicitors who were reluctant to carry out the work due to its 'distasteful character'.[14] Alternatives were considered, such as paying for a service (for example by means of state funding or a levy on the profession) but the committee felt that the voluntary scheme should continue.

> [In] our opinion, there exists a moral obligation on the part of the profession, in return for the monopoly in the practice of the law which it enjoys, to render gratuitous legal assistance to those members of the community who cannot afford to pay for such assistance, provided that no undue burden is thereby cast upon any individual members of the profession ... The evidence given before us shows that this moral obligation is fully recognised.

It is an interesting comment and reveals a shift from pro bono as an expression of chivalrous or Christian charitable motives to one of professional responsibility. The profession's obligation to undertake pro bono services was expressed as a quid pro quo for its professional monopoly. The committee recommended variously that the administration of the scheme should be transferred from the Poor Persons department in the Royal Courts of Justice to the Law Society, the state should pay a grant to support the administrative costs, and the courts in assize towns (those eight towns where High Court judges would sit) should be able to hear cases. This was a boost to the status of the Law Society and to solicitors in general. However there was an undercurrent in the Lawrence report that reflects the professional rivalry between the Bar and solicitors.

Lawrence did not recommend extending the jurisdiction of the county court to hear divorce cases where solicitors had rights of audience. Jurisdiction remained in the High Court, albeit with some decentralisation of powers to the registries and the eight assize towns.[15] As a consequence barristers kept their monopoly on advocacy in divorce cases and many people were prevented from divorcing because the costs and inconvenience of having to go to London or one of the assize towns was prohibitive. That limitation on jurisdiction was a source of great discontent amongst people seeking divorce and solicitors alike.

The Findlay report

In April 1925 the Lord Chancellor, Viscount Cave and the Home Secretary, Sir William Johnston-Hicks, appointed a committee to look into 'what facilities exist for giving to poor persons advice with respect to their legal rights and liabilities, and aid in the conduct of legal proceedings whether civil or criminal ... and to report what, if any, further steps should be taken in respect of these matters'.[16]

Divorce and other proceedings in the High Court were excluded from the committee's remit as these were already within the scope of the existing Poor Persons procedure. There was disagreement over this as well as other issues in the final committee report on civil. This led to a further dissenting report by two members of the committee in which they called for the extension of the Poor Persons Rules to the county courts.[17]

Two official reports were published. The first on criminal legal aid was published in March 1926 and was supported by all the committee members. It recommended that the requirement for defendants to disclose their defence in advance should be scrapped and that in limited circumstances magistrates should be given the power to grant legal aid. This led four years later to the Poor Persons Defence Act 1930, mentioned previously.

A second official report for civil was published in 1928 along with the dissenting report. Both reports recognised that the social legislation that had been introduced by the government prior to the First World War had increased the need for civil legal advice. Bills introducing health insurance, education, unemployment benefit, pensions, and support for the sick and infirm had been passed by the Liberal government in the period 1906 to 1914. The bills had been supported in parliament by the Liberal Party and the then fledgling Labour Party.

Political attitudes towards the role of the state were changing. In 1909 the then Chancellor of the Exchequer, Lloyd George, had introduced a budget that for the first time had sought to redistribute wealth. The attempt by the House of Lords to reject the budget eventually led to the Parliament Act 1911, which redefined the powers of the Lords. Such reforms were largely a response to social change, most significantly the enfranchisement of the working class. Expectations regarding the state's involvement in the provision of services were changing.

The committee heard evidence from, among others, one 'Miss E A Berthen', a solicitor who had founded two Poor Man's Lawyer services. Berthen argued that without access to a lawyer people were in danger of feeling powerless and this could lead to discontent and the disintegration of society. She proposed that Poor Man's Lawyer services should be available to all and, to prevent profiteering by unscrupulous solicitors, lawyers should be debarred from taking fees in such cases.

In the official report the committee paid a fulsome tribute to lawyers like Berthen who were providing the pro bono services. It appealed to the Law Society and the Bar to establish services where none existed, but it did not see the need to devote public funds to the work. In responding to a witness who had used the analogy of health to argue for a 'Legal Hospital System', the committee argued that while it was in the state's interests for people to be healthy it was not necessarily in its interest for them to be litigious.

The dissenting report published by two members of the committee was more radical. It argued that the need for advice could not be met by a voluntary service as, due to the expansion of social legislation, there would be a concurrent increase in the numbers of poor people seeking advice. They suggested that lawyers should be employed by local councils to give advice. The service would be paid for from local taxes or the Exchequer, as was the case with the Medical Officer for Health.

Welsh revolt and the collapse of the Poor Persons Rules

The Findlay committee failed to recognise that the voluntary scheme was inadequate to meet the burgeoning demand for legal advice. In the years before the Second World War, the Poor Persons scheme collapsed under the weight of this demand and the independent Poor Man's Lawyer services continued to meet only a fraction of the need for non-family civil legal advice.

Solicitors were divided on whether a voluntary service under the Poor Persons procedure, administered by the Law Society, should continue. Solicitors in London dominated the Law Society and they rejected a suggestion by the government that solicitors should be paid a set fee for divorce cases for poor people as they believed it would be 'undignified to convert what had been instituted as charity into a poorly paid business'.[18] Provincial law societies thought otherwise. Due to the change in divorce law introduced by the Matrimonial Causes Act 1937, which widened the grounds on which divorce could be granted, demand was far outstripping the supply of pro bono services. Solicitors continued to be unhappy about the restriction of divorce hearings to the High Court as it made these less accessible and excluded solicitors from representing clients.

The Law Societies of Wales were especially strident in their opposition to providing services under the Poor Persons procedure. Their practices were often based in areas where there were high levels of poverty and the numbers of potential clients unable to pay for divorce cases far exceeded the numbers who could. In June 1939, following the lead of the members of the Swansea Law Society who had been striking for a year, the Associated Law Societies of Wales agreed not to undertake any further cases until reasonable fees were paid and rules on which courts could hear cases were reformed.

Faced with the hostility of many provincial solicitors and the outright rebellion against the scheme by Welsh solicitors, the government decided that drastic action was called for. They formed a committee. The permanent secretary to the Lord Chancellor, Claud

Schuster, wrote to Mr Justice Hodson, asking him to chair the committee. In his letter he suggested that, subject to treasury approval, lawyers should be paid for carrying out the work. Thus it can be argued that the idea for a state-funded legal aid service did not originate with the Law Society, which eventually administered the scheme, but with the government. Hodson's committee never sat as history intervened.

From September 1939 Britain was at war with Nazi Germany. Wartime conditions led to recognition that the armed forces and civilian population needed access to advice on a range of civil problems. To meet this demand Citizens Advice Bureaux and voluntary legal advice sessions within the armed services were established. By the end of 1942, a legal aid scheme for armed services personnel had been organised. The Law Society established a salaried solicitor service called the 'Service Divorce Department'. It dealt with divorce cases for service personnel in the lower ranks for a fee of three guineas paid for by the government. With many solicitors serving in the armed forces and therefore unable to provide pro bono services, the Law Society was forced to drop its objections to a paid service. By the beginning of 1944 it employed five solicitors out of a staff of about 60 including a section dealing with civilian cases.

The preface to a book called *Legal Aid* published in 1945 chronicles how the wartime experience had effectively embedded a growing legal advice sector. Professor AL Goodhart wrote:

> It was not only in the Services that legal advice was found necessary ... [The] various citizens' advice bureaux which were established to help civilians with their wartime difficulties were flooded with questions concerning legal problems. It was difficult to deal with these by voluntary help alone because the amount of work was more than could be dealt with in spare time hours, so two Legal Advice Centres with salaried staffs had been established in London. It is hardly conceivable that these will now be closed after the war as they have shown how essential this service is to the poor.

Pro bono work today

Law firms, barristers, the voluntary sector and law schools carry on the pro bono tradition. There is a strong sense of altruism and professional duty that motivates many lawyers to undertake this work. It also helps many at the beginning of their careers gain experience and, of course, it has a great public relations value. A substantial amount of work is undertaken on a pro bono basis. A survey of 1,001 solicitors firms conducted by the Law Society in 2007 found that 51 per cent participated in pro bono work. Based on the survey the Law Society estimated that the equivalent of £338 million, 2 per cent of the total fee income for the firms participating in pro bono work, was given. There is, however, no breakdown as to what that value constitutes in terms of work.

But as many commentators, from LAG to the pioneer of the Poor Man's Lawyer movement, Gurney-Champion, recognised, pro bono work cannot be a substitute for a properly funded state system of legal aid. It is a point that today's growing pro bono movement is keen to stress. The influential organisation LawWorks, which organises pro bono rotas in voluntary organisations and promotes pro bono in the UK specifies in its protocol: 'pro bono legal work is always only an adjunct to, and not a substitute for, a proper system of publicly funded legal services'.

In very recent years, pro bono has been elevated from its informal professional pastime status to a significant source of legal help. The London office of Clifford Chance (the world's biggest law firm) was reported to have written off nearly £10 million of work recorded to pro bono files in 2006/07.

Pro bono has been embraced by the political establishment, having received a government endorsement from New Labour. In 2002 the then Attorney-General, Lord Goldsmith QC (who himself set up a free advice centre in East London's Bethnal Green) set up a pro bono committee, which included the Solicitor-General Harriet Harman who was to become deputy leader of the Labour party. Harman started her career as an adviser at Brent Law Centre.

Unsurprisingly there has been some scepticism at the enthusiasm of a government for pro bono which has presided over a period of retreat for publicly funded legal services. Michael Napier QC, senior partner at the claimant firm Irwin Mitchell and former Law Society president, was appointed Attorney-General's pro bono envoy. Napier has been tireless in stressing that pro bono is 'an adjunct to, and not a substitute for' legal aid.

At the end of 2008 the launch of a new initiative called the Access to Justice Foundation marked another milestone in the movement. The organisation is to be the beneficiary of money raised through the Legal Services Act 2007 s194. This is an unprecedented statutory arrangement that effectively allows courts in England and Wales to require a party who loses a legal case against a party in a pro bono case to make a payment to the foundation in an amount equal to an order for costs. Previously, the position under the law was that a losing party would have had no liability to cover costs despite the fact that they, if successful, would have been able to recover costs. The foundation will work with 'regional legal support trusts' whose task will be to direct funds to the not-for-profit sector to locate local need.

This is a positive development. LAG's concern is that the line between pro bono and the government's commitment to funding advice services adequately is strictly policed. In other words that this new enterprise does not become a mechanism whereby the City, through its pro bono endeavours, bails out an increasingly impoverished not-for-profit advice sector.

1   M Cappelletti and J Gordley, 'Legal aid: modern theme and variations' [1972] *Stanford Law Review* 347.
2   See Robert Egerton, *Legal aid*, Kegan Paul, 1945, pp6ff.
3   Michael Zander, *Legal services for the community*, Temple Smith, 1978, p16.
4   Geoffrey Robertson, *The tyrannicide brief*, Chatto & Windus, 2005.
5   Robert Egerton, *Legal Aid*, Kegan Paul, 1945, p85.
6   Asa Briggs and Anne Macartney, *Toynbee Hall: the first hundred years*, Routledge & Kegan Paul, 1984, p9.
7   FCG Gurney Champion, *Justice and the poor in England*, Routledge, 1926, p16.
8   Gurney Champion, note 7 above, p23.
9   Egerton, note 2 above, p147.
10 *Report of the Royal Commission on Divorce and Matrimonial Causes* Cd 6478, HMSO, 1912.
11 *Report of the Prescribed Officers in connection with the Poor Persons Procedure* J153/1, 1915.
12 Lawrence Stone, *Road to divorce: England 1530–1987*, Clarendon, 1990, p435.
13 *Report of the Committee to Enquire Into the Poor Persons Rules* Cmd 430, 1919, para 9.
14 *Report of the Poor Persons Rules Committee* Cmd 2358, 1925.
15 *Report of the Poor Persons Rules Committee*, note 14 above, p10.
16 Warrant of appointment to the Finlay committee, 7 April 1925.
17 Minority report of Dorothy Jewson and Rhys J Davies, para 5.
18 Meeting of the Poor Persons Rules Committee, 21 October 1938 (Law Society Committee Minutes, vol 11 p72).

CHAPTER 2

Legal aid: the most friendless wing of the welfare state

After the Second World War, legal aid moved from its pro bono origins to a publicly funded service provided by private practice law firms and not-for-profit agencies. As discussed in the previous chapter, a limited state-funded legal aid scheme had been established in the criminal courts in the first half of the 20th century, but there was no equivalent civil scheme.

Lord Rushcliffe was a former Conservative MP who had practised as a barrister. In 1944 Rushcliffe was asked to form a committee to look into establishing a legal aid system. The work of the committee was in keeping with the mood of the times. As the country struggled in its battle with fascism, it was recognised that policies needed to be developed to give people hope that the post-conflict world would be worth the sacrifices of war. On a more practical point, it was clear that the Poor Persons Rules were not working and that opinion was shifting away from viewing pro bono services as being adequate to provide legal advice to the poor. The dissenting report from the 1928 Findlay committee, arguing that the state should step in to fund legal aid, was becoming the prevailing view. Political thought reflected this and, for example, the Haldane Society of Socialist Lawyers (an independent group of left wing lawyers founded in 1930) in its submission to the Rushcliffe committee argued that for the poor to depend on charity for legal advice was 'wrong in principle and does not in practice work'. The Law Society, which had been running the Service Divorce department during the war (see Chapter 1), also moved from its previous position of calling for voluntary services only.

William Beveridge's 1942 report, *Social Insurance and Allied Services*, had called on the state to fight the five 'giant evils': want, disease, ignorance, squalor and idleness. Beveridge was strongly influenced by the experience of the economic depression in the 1930s which had financially ruined many and was a contributing factor in the rise of fascism on the continent. His report led to the establishment of what became known as the welfare state, based upon four pillars:

- a National Health Service;
- universal housing;
- state security (welfare benefits); and
- universal education.

The main recommendations of Rushcliffe's final report were in keeping with this radical vision. As far as a system of publicly funded law was concerned, he recommended:

- legal aid should be available in those types of case in which lawyers normally represented private individual clients;
- legal aid should not be limited to those people 'normally classed as poor' but should include those of 'small or moderate means';
- there should be an increasing scale of contributions payable by those with income or capital above minimum levels, below which legal aid would be free;
- in addition to the means test, cases should be subject to a merit test, designed to be judged by legal practitioners independent of government, on a similar basis to those applied to private clients;
- legal aid should be funded by the state but administered by the Law Society. The Lord Chancellor should be the minister responsible, assisted by an advisory committee; and
- 'adequate' remuneration should be paid to barristers and solicitors working under the scheme.

Salaried services were suggested by some groups as the way forward. The Poor Man's Lawyer movement suggested such a service to tackle the housing, debt and benefit problems faced by poorer communities. The Haldane Society argued that the Citizens Advice Bureaux network, which had been established during the war, could form the basis of a salaried lawyer legal aid system.

Rushcliffe, though, largely accepted what the Law Society had proposed to the committee, which was for a legal aid scheme provided by solicitors in private practice and, where appropriate, barristers. The Law Society was concerned to wind up the salaried service divorce department, believing the department 'presented too much of a threat for practitioners'.[1] It was also keen for solicitors to re-establish their practices in the aftermath of the war and saw the legal aid scheme as a way to help achieve that goal.

Justice delayed: the first 20 years

The period from 1950 when the legal aid scheme was introduced to 1970 represents the foundation period of the legal aid scheme that we know today. Not everyone was convinced, even in the judiciary. Within the first year, Lord Justice Singleton said that he was 'rather appalled at the number of assisted persons there are'. He also expressed the hope that it 'will not mean the disappearance of the ordinary litigant'.[2] While the original Legal Aid Act was framed very much with the Rushcliffe principles at its core, spending restraints limited the service from the start. Up until the 1970s the scheme was mainly used for supporting civil litigation relating to family law and defending people accused of a crime. For example, a survey of legally-aided cases in Birmingham in 1969 found that 86 per cent were for family matters.[3] Criminal legal aid expenditure increased in this period, especially after the Widgery report in 1966 which led to legal aid becoming the norm for people accused of crimes before the magistrates' courts.

In 1950 it was reckoned that 80 per cent of the population was entitled to civil legal aid on the means test and the trend has been for successive governments to erode eligibility. By 1973 it had collapsed to 40 per cent of the population, and was down to an all-time low of 29 per cent in 2008. This decline has been accompanied by reductions in both scope as well as rates paid to lawyers (see Chapter 5). Such measures were all aimed at controlling expenditure.

By 1969, some £6 million was being spent on civil legal aid and the same sum was being spent on criminal legal aid in the lower courts. Higher court criminal legal aid continued to be paid separately until April 2003 (see Chapter 3). In its 20th annual report on the scheme the Law Society in 1969 acknowledged the shortcomings of legal aid, arguing that an advisory service should be added to the scheme as the original Act had intended. This had not been implemented due to 'economic problems'. The report also noted that the government did not intend to extend legal aid to the new industrial tribunals (now employment tribunals), and called for the government to look at 'some form of ancillary legal services, of persons with some legal and sociological training' to support clients in the tribunal system.

In this foundation period, the development of legal aid was sty-mied for much the same reasons it faces today. In the early years, the government could fairly cite economic difficulties as a reason not to increase the budget as victory in the war had come at a high price. While this could be said to be true for the last two years of the 1945–51 Labour administrations, it could not be applied to most of the 1950s and 1960s as the country experienced solid economic growth for much of this period. The problem for legal aid was – and remains – that it did not enjoy the same political priority as health, education and other public services.

The *Guardian* columnist, Jonathan Freedland, mindful of the 2006 Carter reforms, neatly summed up legal aid's place in the wel-fare state and its vulnerability to budget cuts.

> [The government] enjoys a powerful advantage, taking on what is surely the most friendless wing of the welfare state. Unlike schools or hospitals, legal aid seems technical and remote to all but those who've had to use it. Its clients are not children or the sick, who arouse our sympathy, but – in one half of the system at least – those accused of crimes. Its advocates are not cherished nurses or admired doctors, but a breed we love to hate in all but their TV drama incarnations: lawyers.[4]

That said, by the late 1960s forces were in fact pushing legal aid up the political agenda. Policy makers and pressure groups increas-ingly recognised that the Rushcliffe model of 'legal aid' was failing poorer communities, and this led to the publication of two influential papers from the Labour and Conservative parties, *Justice for All* by the Society of Labour Lawyers in 1968 and *Rough Justice* published by the Conservative Party. The latter argued that the legal system had to reach out to the poor in order to remedy 'the failure of many people who need legal advice to ever get to a solicitor's office'. Legal academ-ics and activists at the time were also influenced by the setting up in the 1960s of 'neighbourhood law offices' in the United States as part of President Johnson's *War on Poverty* programme. This led to the proposal for the establishment of law centres staffed by solicitors.

Justice for all

While Rushcliffe rejected alternatives to the private practice model, the 'not-for-profit' idea persisted along with a growing view which be-lieved that legal aid should target more directly the problems faced by impoverished communities. Voluntary services such as those from the pre-war Poor Man's Lawyer era continued as a parallel service to legal aid. The most important of the voluntary services by virtue of size was the Citizens Advice Bureaux.

The National Council for Voluntary Services had established bureaux as part of the war effort to disseminate information to the public. When war broke out in September 1939, 200 bureaux were immediately established and by 1945 there were over 1,000. In contrast to previous voluntary legal advice services, bureaux offered, as a matter of principle, services to everyone regardless of their means. After the war the number of bureaux was reduced by half when government funding to the national organisation in the form of a grant was lost in 1953. Despite lack of central government funding, the numbers of enquiries dealt with by them had reached a million by 1966. From the mid-1960s the number of bureaux increased to 869 by 1986.

In 1973 the government renewed the grant to the National Association of Citizens Advice Bureaux (NACAB). At present Citizens Advice, as the national organisation is now called, receives around £45 million in central government support and the local bureaux have an income of £141 million, mainly from local authorities. As discussed in Chapter 3, the Legal Services Commission has become an increasingly important funder and currently has contracts worth £30 million with bureaux. Throughout the 1970s and 1980s the service became an increasingly powerful force in the voluntary advice sector. Citizens Advice ensures bureau quality standards and co-ordinates social policy work. While some of the larger urban bureaux developed specialisms in social welfare law, they have tended not to employ lawyers (who are able to litigate cases).

One of the reasons that voluntary services have grown in the UK (as opposed to other jurisdictions) is that the provision of legal advice to the public is not restricted to lawyers (apart from advice on immigration law).

Non-lawyer services have grown in the private sector as well. In many tribunals a legal qualification is not required to represent clients and so, for example, in employment tribunals both solicitors and non-lawyer claims companies represent employees and employers. However, in other courts, lawyers' rights of audience are required and so only qualified lawyers have the authority to conduct litigation on behalf of clients. Clients might have been able to get some initial advice but would not have access to legal advice if they needed to take their case further. This was a particular problem in housing and public law cases in the 1960s and early 1970s as clients could get advice from a citizens advice bureau or other non-lawyer service but would not be able to take their case to court. Law centres employ solicitors and are therefore able to conduct litigation on behalf of clients.

The idea of a network for national law centres was first conceived of 40 years ago as a radical alternative to existing provision. 'Nothing less than the introduction of a new public service to operate along-side, and in supplement to, the private profession would suffice to deal adequately with the problem of providing proper legal services to a section of the public who went short of them,' wrote Michael Zander QC, emeritus professor of law at the London School of Economics, about law centres in 1978. Zander was the first person in this country to write about and commend US-style neighbourhood law firms.[5] He was also the main author of the Society of Labour Lawyers' seminal pamphlet, *Justice for All* (1968), which led directly to the establishment of the first law centre two years later.

The law centre movement was 'a radical attempt to change the delivery of legal services', wrote the former LAG director Roger Smith, currently director of the legal and human rights organisation Justice.[6] Smith joined Camden Law Centre in 1973 before becoming director of West Hampstead in 1975. 'The idea was that law centres were going to be about systematic change and not just "band-aid" legal services', he said. 'These were organisations that through their work in the community and their work in the courts wanted to change the world. It was highly idealistic.'

The law centre movement would dump 'the formality and staid dignity of the typical solicitors' office' and 'present an informal, casual atmosphere', wrote Zander. The idea behind the law centre was to take the law to the people who needed it but previously had been denied it. So law centres would occupy the high streets and shopping centres with shop-front exteriors – as opposed to discreet brass name plaques – boldly declaring themselves: 'Law Centres'.

The look and feel of a law centre was to be very different. Office walls would be festooned with posters promoting housing rights, support for battered wives and campaigns for racial equality. As Zander noted, the furniture tended towards the 'somewhat dilapidated' and the lawyers and support staff 'all tend to wear jeans and unconventional hairstyles'. The spirit of the law centres (not to mention the furniture and some of the haircuts) remains unchanged.

The first law centre had been set up in a former butcher's shop premises in North Kensington, London. It was opened in July 1970 on Golborne Road at the very north end of Portobello Road. This was pre-Hugh Grant Notting Hill where the new immigrants rubbed along uneasily with white working class communities living in substandard housing, much of it provided by notorious landlords like Peter Rachman. It was a world vividly captured in a 1974 *World in Action* film called 'Law Shop', which bluntly labelled the semi-derelict network of terrace houses in the shadow of then new A40 West Way a 'slum area'.

The opening of the centre in 1970 was presided over by the president of the Law Society, Godfrey Morley, and the Labour Attorney-General, Sir Elwyn Jones, with personal messages of support from the Lord Chancellor, Lord Hailsham and chairman of the Law Commission, Sir Leslie Scarman.

In keeping with the law centres that followed, North Kensington was accountable to the community it served through a management committee elected from local people. The founding of the movement challenged the legal establishment and the Law Society was initially hostile to its development. Solicitors in private practice felt threatened by what amounted to a salaried legal service.

In 1973 the Law Society in its annual report decried the movement's core ethos of 'responsibility to their local communities' as a subversive means of 'stirring up political and quasi-political confrontation far removed from ensuring equal access to the protection of the law'. That same year Chancery Lane secured its own advice and assistance scheme sanctioned by the government, which became the 'green form' scheme. It provided that advice on any matter of law could be made available on the basis of a simplified means test carried out by the solicitor.

The Society effectively controlled the law centres by conditions attached to the 'waiver' required by solicitors to be employed in law centres. There was a stand-off in 1975 over the establishment of Hillingdon Law Centre. A deal was brokered whereby the not-for-profit side promised to keep off the private practice patch (such as crime, family work, personal injury, probate and conveyancing). Once that concordat had been reached the law centre movement was up and running and another 13 centres opened between 1973 and 1974.

Law centres mainly developed services in what has become known as 'social welfare' law, including areas of civil law such as welfare rights, immigration, employment, housing, discrimination and public law. This was exactly the type of work which had been called for by the Poor Man's Lawyer movement in their contributions to the Rushcliffe committee. Unemployment reached a peak at over 3.5 million in 1984 and the increase in lone parents as well as a growing awareness of rights amongst disadvantaged groups fed the demand for social welfare law services.

Up to 1982 the Department of the Environment through its Inner Urban Aid Programme funded new law centres and other advice agencies.[7] Increasingly local government became the major funder of social welfare law advice. With this support the number of law centres grew from half a dozen in 1974 to a peak of over 60 in the mid-1980s. This was dwarfed though by the increase in the numbers of citizens advice bureaux and other independent advice centres. By 1986 there were 1,236 generalist advice agencies providing welfare rights and other advice.[8] There were also a few hundred non-welfare rights advice organisations giving advice on housing, immigration and other areas of social welfare law. There has been some fall in numbers mainly caused by cutbacks in spending. Currently, there are 55 law centres, 455 main bureaux working out of 3,300 locations, and just under 1,000 independent advice organisations which are members of the other generalist advice network, Advice UK.

Advice UK was founded in 1979 as the national organisation for the independent advice centres. Its membership comprises large organisations through to small community based groups. The organisation derives much of its income from providing services to members, including professional indemnity insurance. It also fundraises for projects, for example it currently runs a project funded by the national lottery to support and develop its membership.

Many local councils (in addition to the voluntary sector advice services established in the 1970s and 1980s) developed in-house services mainly in welfare rights. By 1997, some 120 local authorities had opened welfare rights services.[9] The establishment of welfare rights and other social welfare law advice services was often linked to local councils' own anti-poverty strategies, an important part of which was to ensure the take-up of benefits and other rights.

A golden period?

If there was a golden period in the history of legal aid in which 'justice for all' appeared an attainable goal rather than a dream, then it was perhaps during the years from 1973 to 1986. Alongside the development of the voluntary sector advice services described above, the period kicked off in 1973 with the establishment of the green form scheme and ended with the implementation of the Police and Criminal Evidence Act in 1986. This was the last major expansion of the legal aid scheme. The Act led to the establishment of the right to legal advice for anyone detained in a police station in recognition of the need for publicly-funded legal advice as a safeguard against miscarriages of justice. Duty schemes in the magistrates' courts were required by law in 1984. These combined with the duty schemes established in police stations, setting the pattern for the provision for criminal defence services which remains to the present day. The expansion of criminal and family legal aid helped fund the growth in firms, and by 1986 legal aid represented 11 per cent of solicitors' incomes (an increase of 5 per cent in ten years).

Under the green form scheme, advice on any matter of English law could be given to a client after the application of a simple means test. As explained before, the scheme had been called for by the Law Society partly to stave off the perceived threat to the private practice model of provision posed by the law centres and other voluntary sector services. In 1982 it was expanded to include representation before mental health review tribunals. Prior to losing office in 1979 the Labour government increased the percentage of the population entitled to claim legal aid to 79 per cent (it was 40 per cent in 1973 at the start of this period).

Despite the introduction of green form legal aid, LAG reported that by 1986 there was only an 11 per cent increase in social welfare law cases being undertaken under the scheme. Over half of the million green forms in 1986 were still for the now traditional core areas of legal aid practice: crime and family. There is a structural bias towards crime and family and away from social welfare law which persists today. It largely suited firms to establish civil practices in family law in this foundation period as it complemented privately-funded divorce work. As criminal legal aid work expanded, firms developed businesses linked to referrals from magistrates' court and police station rotas as well as building up own client work. It should also be acknowledged that increases in the numbers of firms undertaking legal aid work in the late 1970s and early 1980s was caused in part by a recession which led solicitors' firms to seek to diversify in other areas of work including legal aid. Conveyancing, a mainstay of the traditional high street practice, also became less profitable as a result of legislation (the Administration of Justice Act) passed in 1985 ending the solicitors' monopoly on the work.

It was the not-for-profit services described in the preceding section that were more responsive to increasing demand for advice to poorer communities. There were significant exceptions to this among private sector practitioners who developed practices in social welfare law. Some solicitors would also move from careers in law centres or other agencies to private work after developing social welfare law specialisms.

Law Society loses control

The 'justice for all' phase of legal aid came to an abrupt end in March 1986. The figures show that there had been a 50 per cent increase in legal aid expenditure in the previous two years and that the rises outstripped the number of clients served. Cost increases in this period cannot be fully explained by increases in eligibility. In response the government rushed through legislation in a shock move to cut eligibility to legal aid. 'The backdoor nature of this legislation coupled with the complete absence of consultation, has stunned legal services groups accustomed to a more leisurely pace of action (if not complete inaction) by the Lord Chancellor', noted *Legal Action* in March 1986.

Worse was to come. At LAG's annual general meeting in May that year the outlook for legal aid was described simply as 'grim', its administration by the Law Society was described as a 'disaster area', and delegates were worried about the likely outcome of a review of the legal aid system which the government had also ordered.

The review only resulted in minor changes to the green form scheme. It had suggested transferring large parts of the green form scheme to the voluntary sector in an updated version of the ideas put to the Rushcliffe committee, and transferring administration of legal aid to an independent body, both suggestions which were welcomed by LAG at the time. These ideas were shelved.

Citizens Advice rejected the idea of the transfer of legal aid while welcoming the review's recognition of the role of the voluntary sector in legal services. NACAB director Elizabeth Filkin, while personally thought to favour the proposal to shift green form to the service, told LAG that they would 'not be party to any attempt at cost cutting or reducing legal services to the poor'. A critical point of difference for the citizens advice bureaux service in considering taking on green form work was that it would undermine its principle of free access as clients would need to be means tested to qualify.

The rise of the legal aid bureaucrat

With their re-election in 1987, the Conservatives returned to the battleground of legal aid reform. In a surprise move by the Prime Minister, Margaret Thatcher, she appointed Lord Mackay as Lord Chancellor and he continued in office until the Conservatives' loss of power to Labour in 1997. Mackay, a Scottish lawyer with working class roots, was from outside the London-based legal establishment.

Mackay picked up responsibility for a bill to reform legal aid from his predecessor and piloted it through the legislative process to the statute books as the Legal Aid Act 1988. LAG was disappointed with the Act as it gave no statement of purpose about what legal aid was for, but merely saw it as an administrative problem to be solved. The centrepiece of the legislation was the replacement of the Law Society with the Legal Aid Board (LAB) as administrators of the scheme, a move which LAG judged 'uncontroversial'. Moving to a government quango with its own governing board, control of legal aid policy had been snatched from the hands of lawyers. The establishment of the LAB ushered in a new era for legal aid in which the government showed little concern for policy and was largely content for the LAB to get on and run the system. Half of the new board were drawn from business.

The administrative shortcomings of the Law Society-run system clearly needed to be addressed, but there was also concern from LAG about reductions in eligibility as well as the disproportionate amount of expenditure going on crime and family cases while neglecting other work. LAG was also fearful of the viability of fee levels. The Act abolished the old calculation of legal aid fees which had been based on a discounted market rate and gave the Lord Chancellor sole responsibility for setting rates.

Steve Orchard was appointed as the first chief executive of the LAB in December 1988. He had worked his way up the civil service career ladder in the Courts Service starting as a clerk at the age of 17 years in Poole county court. His appointment confirmed the view that the Lord Chancellor had wanted a competent manager to oversee the LAB rather than a lawyer with direct experience of legal services. Orchard's appointment proved crucial as he, together with the Board, came to dominate legal aid policy. 'The Board's command of its brief; its business-dominated approach; its possession of the empirical detail of legal aid and its sheer effectiveness have given it a lead role in policy-making. Much of this strength flows from the force of character of its chief executive since its beginning, Steve Orchard,' wrote LAG's director Roger Smith in 1997.[10]

The Board's dominant role sometimes led to tensions with its parent department. Throughout its history, especially at times of difficulty, LAG has picked up policy differences between the LAB and government. One side usually blames the other for a failed policy initiative. These disagreements though have never spilled over into the public domain to any significant degree. The LAB ran legal aid for the ten years to 1998 when it was superseded by the Legal Services Commission (LSC). In the LSC period of control they have generally moved closer to the government and been less keen to assert their independence.

Control of expenditure was mainly achieved by changing eligibility and scope in civil legal aid. In 1992/93 the percentage of households eligible for civil legal aid was drastically reduced from 77 to 53 per cent and in subsequent years that figure was eaten away, reducing it to levels which made civil legal aid largely a sink service for people on means-tested benefits.

Scope was also restricted. One of Lord Mackay's first moves was to take probate and property advice out of the green form scheme. The political imperative to control the budget largely at the expense of access to justice in this period meant that the bureaucrat was in the ascendant over the lawyers who wanted to expand the system. Steve Orchard described the green form system as 'a problem'. 'Many solicitors were milking the system', he said.[11] The number of green form cases increased by 50 per cent in the ten years to 1997. There was some abuse of the green form system. For example, Midlands based solicitor Alan Pritchard was found guilty in 2000 of defrauding the LAB of £2.25 million and sentenced to five years' imprisonment.

The growth in green form advice can be explained in large part by increasing demand. By the end of the 1990s, citizens advice bureaux were dealing with over 5.5 million problems a year. The 1.5 million green form cases therefore need to seen in this context (albeit that many of the problems bureaux dealt with could be classified as generalist as opposed to legal ones). As LAG has put it: 'There is a massive need for legal advice and an infinite need for general advice'. At its heart the green form scheme was a valiant attempt to ensure access to legal advice on any legal problem. It fell foul of budget constraints and the temptation of some to use it for low level enquiries to maximise profit. Without adequate quality controls the system was open to abuse.

In the LAB period, eligibility and scope were not reduced for criminal legal aid. 'We had to assess and pay the bills for the magistrate's court and police station work,' Steve Orchard said. 'There was no room for any huge policy changes.' The figures throughout the decade to 1998 for the magistrates' court rotas and police station work were stable and £33 million and £82 million respectively by the end. The introduction of standard fees in magistrates' court (see Chapter 7) in 1993 had little impact on costs rising, as they did, in line with inflation. The LAB's major concern was that in both crime and civil legal aid there were too many 'dabblers'. In London, for example, 40 per cent of the firms did 90 per cent of the criminal defence work.

The LAB's main policy initiative was the introduction of franchising. It was originally sold to practitioners as a non-compulsory system of quality assurance which would free them from bureaucratic controls. By April 1997 out of a total of 12,000 legal aid firms a total of 1,740 were franchised. This approach went some way to developing a credible framework for assessing the quality of firms' advice that was previously absent. In franchised firms, management audits were carried out by the LSC against a set of good practice criteria. For the first time quality of public-funded work was checked. Audit included evaluating a firm's policies on independent file review and conflicts of interests, through to personnel policies such as equal opportunities recruitment, professional development and others. Files were audited against model answers known as 'transaction criteria'. This was supposed to check the quality of work for individual clients, but had only partial success in achieving this. Accreditation schemes for family law and police station work were also run in conjunction with the Law Society. In addition to these quality initiatives, the LAB ran a pilot project of 42 voluntary advice agencies requiring them to work to franchise standards.

As chief executive of the LAB and latterly the LSC, Orchard personified the able bureaucrat. He, and the Board, held the whip-hand on legal aid policy rather than the politicians. The genesis of the policies on the key reforms of the quality standards and the opening of legal aid contracting to non-lawyer agencies were not party political in design or implementation. As discussed in the next chapter they were adopted enthusiastically by the incoming New Labour government as a part of a repackaging of legal aid and voluntary advice services.

From Rushcliffe to the LAB

Rushcliffe wanted a legal aid system that would enable the majority of the population to be able to pursue just claims or to defend themselves regardless of means. To achieve this, lawyers would be paid by the state for individual cases. Unfortunately, at the outset this vision foundered on the rocks of economic hardship and the vested interests of lawyers. For much of its history, criminal and family cases have dominated expenditure on legal aid, mainly for the dual reasons of demand and the pattern of private practice provision.

The foundation period of legal aid was followed by a period of expansion. In the late 1960s it was recognised that legal aid was not

serving impoverished communities. Parallel social welfare law services that had developed in the voluntary sector were often more
effective in meeting the needs of these communities. Progress was
made towards ensuring 'justice for all' in the period 1973 to 1986
with the widening of access to legal aid for people accused of a crime
and the introduction of the green form scheme in civil legal aid.

In the LAB period of development there were improvements in
the administration of legal aid, but there was little political vision
about what the system was for. This period saw the increasing use of
scope and eligibility cuts, particularly in civil legal aid, to control the
budget at the expense of access to justice.

1   *The future of publicly funded legal services*, Law Society, 2003, p34.
2   Michael Zander, *Legal services for the community*, Temple Smith, 1978.
3   L Bridges, B Sufin, J Whetton and R Whie, *Legal services in Birmingham*,
    Birmingham University, 1975.
4   *Guardian* 11 October 2006.
5   *Socialist Commentary* September 1966.
6   *Independent Lawyer* April 2007.
7   Mike Stephens, *Community law centres: a critical appraisal*, Avebury, 1990,
    p114.
8   Richard Berthoud, Sheila Benson and Sandra Williams, *Standing up for
    claimants*, Policy Studies Institute, 1986.
9   Neil Bateman, *Practising welfare rights*, Routledge, 2006, p21.
10 Roger Smith, *Justice: redressing the balance*, LAG, 2007, p33.
11 LAG interview with Steve Orchard, May 2008.

CHAPTER 3

New Labour: papering over the cracks

New Labour's approach to legal aid has fallen into two distinct periods, or to use a familiar footballers' phrase, it has so far been a game of two halves. Looking back over the first decade of New Labour, these two periods have been determined by the radically different approaches of the last two Lord Chancellors.

Lord Irvine's period in the office of Lord Chancellor, from the start of the New Labour administration to his abrupt departure in June 2003, was – in the context of legal aid policy – radical stuff. Irvine might have been unpopular with the profession, nonetheless this period represented an unprecedented attempt to seize control of publicly funded law. It was informed by a coherent vision of a 'Community Legal Service' (CLS) under a new Legal Services Commission (LSC). The success, or not, of that vision is assessed later in Chapter 5. However, it should be acknowledged that the CLS was a flagship policy of New Labour and an attempt to grasp a nettle dodged by previous administrations in its ambition to co-ordinate a raggedly disparate landscape of providers. Irvine was prepared to be controversial as well by, as he put it, 'facing down the vested interests'. It was Lord Irvine who removed personal injury from legal aid, leaving the fate of accident victims to the mercy of market forces and enhanced 'no win, no fee' deals. It was a huge gamble.

History will treat the more personable Lord Falconer less kindly. He possessed no such vision of publicly funded legal services. Access to justice, as far as it impinged on the public purse, was dealt with in policy terms as a problem to be contained. His vision was unwaveringly aligned to that of the Treasury and, in particular, how best to control the runaway train of criminal legal aid spending. The 'fundamental' legal aid review was superseded by the Carter review.

Budgetary constraints led to a retrenchment of the legal aid administration into a centralised London-based service in which an agenda
of cost-cutting and competitive tendering was pursued.

Because Britain deserves better

The relative backwater of public expenditure that is legal aid (total
expenditure on legal aid is currently only enough to run the National
Health Service for two weeks) needs to be seen in the wider political
context that led to New Labour coming to power in June 1997 after
18 years in opposition. Any incoming government brings with it the
hope of change even though hope, in the world of publicly-funded
law, had been a commodity in short supply. Labour's acceptance of
the previous administration's spending limits meant there was no
realistic expectation of any great change in the budget for legal aid.

Labour's caution was mainly due to their defeat in the 1992 general election. They had expected to win, or at least gain sufficient
seats to lead to a hung Parliament. However, the Conservatives led
by John Major limped through with a majority of 21 seats sufficient
to sustain his government for a full term. Part of that success was the
Conservatives' record on the economy. When faced with the choice
of electing a government, it seemed the electorate trusted the Tories
more than Labour to run the economy.

The Conservatives had been successful in exploiting the problems
of the last Labour government to create a narrative of economic incompetence. This was symbolised by the 1978 'winter of discontent'
with its public sector strikes and harsh economic climate contributing to widespread disaffection with the government. To counter this,
Labour rebranded itself 'New Labour', signalling a break with the
past and declaring that it would for the first two years work within
the Tories' budget.

Labour was also helped by 'Black Wednesday'. In September 1992,
the Conservative chancellor Norman Lamont was forced to abandon
the exchange rate mechanism linking the pound's value to the euro.
Lamont had fought a forlorn battle against the money markets at a
cost of £27 billion to defend the pound's value, leading to interest
rates spiralling to 15 per cent at one point in mid-September. The
debacle was seized upon by New Labour to turn the tables on the
Conservatives, accusing them of economic incompetence.

By June 1997, the economic conditions were better, partly helped
by the better trading figures that a devalued pound had brought about,

but the mood of the country had swung decisively against the Conservatives and they were swept from office. Labour returned to power with a majority of 177 seats, the largest they had ever enjoyed.

Central to the New Labour message was that it was not wedded to the old ideology. For much of the period up to 1979, while Labour governments tended to increase public spending more than Conservative ones, a political consensus prevailed surrounding the maintenance of the post-war welfare state. That consensus had been broken by the election of Margaret Thatcher's Conservative government in 1979 which aimed to reduce taxation and state spending on services. Central to this was the introduction of market competition in public services through competitive tendering. New Labour, as well as accepting the outgoing government's spending limits, also wanted to regulate the cost and delivery of public services through market competition.

Not so much New Labour, as Old Treasury

The first phase of New Labour's stewardship of legal aid was presided over by Lord Derry Irvine of Lairg who became Lord Chancellor when Labour came to power. Irvine had been Tony Blair's old pupil master in the early years of his legal career. The connection between the two was also personal. Irvine was credited with introducing him to his future wife Cherie Booth. She was a trainee barrister in the same chambers, 11 King's Bench Walk, where Irvine was head. It had been widely anticipated that he would become Lord Chancellor when his former pupil became Prime Minister. It would be wrong though to portray this as simply a matter of cronyism. His previous links to the Blairs would certainly have been no impediment to his promotion, but Irvine had a long history of involvement with Labour predating Blair's leadership. When Labour had been in opposition, Irvine had been shadow Lord Chancellor for five years. He was appointed by the previous Labour leader John Smith, whom he had befriended in his student days at Glasgow University.

In opposition Labour had been vague about its plans for legal aid. In its manifesto for the 1997 election, *New Labour: because Britain deserves better*, Labour promised to establish a 'Community Legal Service', introduce better regional planning of services and have a wide ranging review of legal aid. At the time, LAG was critical of both the Conservatives and Labour. 'Both the government and the Labour opposition have stitched themselves into a corner. In just over two years' time, both have committed themselves to making real cuts in expenditure to a program that is rising at 10 per cent a year.' LAG argued that eligibility and scope should be extended as far as possible within the budgetary constraints and argued against a hard cap that would prevent expenditure going over the allocated budget.

The sector was caught on the back foot by the new Lord Chancellor as he announced radical plans for the reform of legal aid at the Law Society's annual conference in October 1997. In his speech he outlined plans to take most civil cases out of the legal aid scheme. Family cases would remain in the scheme. Those other cases in the future would be funded by 'no win, no fee' deals, or conditional fee agreements. In an attempt to portray this move as widening access to justice to the middle classes no longer eligible for legal aid, the proposals were trailed in the *Mail on Sunday* and the *Times*. Sir Peter Middleton's report on legal aid was published to accompany Lord Irvine's Cardiff speech and affirmed that all legal aid money claims could be replaced by conditional fees.[1] 'Excluding claims for money or damages from legal aid will put those on low income, as well as those on middle or higher incomes on an equal footing – taking forward a civil case will depend on whether or not it has merit to persuade a lawyer to handle it on a "no win, no fee" basis,' Lord Irvine told delegates.

At the time commentators opposed the move, believing clients previously on legal aid would lose compensation by having to pay legal and insurance costs from any compensation awarded. The move was viewed as a blatant attempt to save money rather than to increase access to justice. The *Financial Times* described the proposals as 'not so much New Labour but Old Treasury'. Consumer groups opposed the move arguing that, due to the cost of insurance premiums to cover the other side's costs, many of the poorest would be excluded or risk having large amounts of their compensation eaten up by lawyers' costs. LAG estimated as much as £100 million in compensation would be lost by 75,000 people whose cases were currently funded by legal aid. Personal injury specialists were caught in a cleft stick over the proposals as they had argued for the introduction of conditional fees for private client work. Whilst the extension of 'no win, no fee' deals commanded some anxious headlines, Irvine made other announcements in a speech that firmly set the direction for the first phase of New Labour's policy on legal aid. Contracts with fixed prices for blocks of work were proposed for all civil and criminal work and a tightening of the merits test as well as the establishment of the CLS.

The CLS was intended to co-ordinate existing services such as citizens advice bureaux, law centres and other voluntary sector advice agencies. Irvine told delegates he wanted the CLS to facilitate 'the refocusing of the legal aid scheme as a tool to help poor people solve social welfare problems by gaining access to the justice system'. To this end, key to Irvine's CLS was an attempt to engage the third sector. Under his Lord Chancellorship, the numbers of not-for-profit agencies holding franchises grew from the initial 42 pilots started under Lord Mackay's previous tenure to over 400 franchises by 2002–03.

Lord Irvine's incendiary speech (at least, by the rather sedate standards of Law Society conferences) also included announcements on Lord Woolf's proposals for the reform of civil justice and separately, in an echo of the Henry VII statute described in Chapter 1, an exemption was allowed from court fees for people on means-tested benefits. The Woolf reforms were intended to reduce the 'cost, delay and complexity' of civil court proceedings.[2] These new rules established the current Civil Procedure Rules introducing protocols before starting court action, more active case management by the courts (including strict timetables for the preparation of cases), the wider use of alternative dispute resolution, as well as the division of cases into 'fast-track' for those under £15,000 in value and 'multi-track' for those above. On the whole the reforms worked well with more cases being settled prior to issuing court proceedings post-Woolf, though this has had the effect of loading more costs onto pre-court work.[3]

Papering over the cracks

Lord Irvine's speech to the Law Society conference set the tone for relations with the legal profession over the implementation of the government's legal aid reforms. Throughout his time as Lord Chancellor, Irvine was characterised as being arrogant and bullying. At the Cardiff event he did little to woo the profession and his refusal to take questions from the floor incensed delegates. However, his solicitor-audience at Cardiff did not forget its professional decorum. As one commentator noted, 'he was somewhat lucky to escape merely with a reduced ovation'.

Irvine's personal commitment to the reforms should not be underestimated. Steve Orchard, chief executive of the Legal Aid Board (LAB) at the time, in an interview given for this book in 2008, describes Irvine as being 'really engaged with legal aid', unlike his predecessor Lord McKay. Orchard personally had over 50 meetings with him. 'Irvine was the one who really got to grips with it,' he said, although he conceded that Irvine and New Labour could have done more to 'sell the policy'. Orchard also confirmed that the initiative to take personal injury out of legal aid came from the ministers, not the LAB. However there was no resistance from the LAB because, as Orchard said, 'there had to be some prioritisation of what legal aid would pay for .... It was always by far the least worst option to save money'.

Orchard also revealed that competitive tendering in legal services was a New Labour innovation, not an ideological hangover from the Tory period. Instead, Orchard said that the LAB, pre-Irvine, backed franchising because they were 'driven by the analysis they had no control over quality' and due to the lack of control over expenditure 'they had no room for huge policy changes'.

It was not just lawyers, whose concerns could be dismissed as an expression of self-interest, who opposed reform. A comment piece in the *Independent* was a fairly typical response:

> The legal aid budget will be restricted to cases in which compensation is not sought, such as criminal cases, injunctions or judicial review. The problem is this will not work. Under a 'no win, no fee' system, the loser in a court case still has to pay the winner's costs. Lord Irvine argues that lawyers should insure themselves against these costs but that will be a business decision about risk and complexity – not about justice.[4]

'No win, no fee' would be brought in for all personal injury claims apart from medical negligence cases. Pressure groups had successfully argued that due to the high costs of investigating medical negligence claims it would have been impossible for potential claimants to find solicitors willing to take the cases on.

'We want to focus tax payers' money where it is most needed and do the most good: on social welfare matters – employment, housing, debt, state benefits and actions against officialdom and bureaucracy,' Irvine said.[5] In defending the proposals before the House of Lords, Irvine argued that the extension of conditional fee agreements would result in £69 million being made available for social welfare law cases in 1999/2000, rising to £100 million by the following year (see Chapter 6). At the same time, he also floated the idea of extending legal aid to employment tribunals. This proposal was predictably met with protests from employers and was eventually dropped.

Both the Bar Council and the Law Society objected to the proposals on personal injury cases. They were joined by a coalition of professional bodies and consumer groups, including LAG, opposing the changes. The then Law Society President, Phillip Sycamore, said that the abolition of legal aid would 'hit poorer litigants hard. Conditional fee agreements may help some clients who will be denied legal aid, but they will not be able to help all. There will be many people with deserving cases who will be denied justice'. The proposals were also condemned by the Conservative party opposition. Conservative MP Edward Garnier called them 'socially divisive, economically illiterate and politically inept'.

Irvine – gaffe-prone, politically naïve and aloof – proved an easy target. Almost every profile of the man makes reference to his infamous defence of the refurbishment of his official apartments in the House of Lords. Irvine attempted to suggest that taxpayers should be grateful that he was spending £650,000 of their money on the project, including wallpaper in the style of Augustus Pugin at the cost of nearly £60,000. For critics defending cash-strapped legal aid this was an open goal. For example, one correspondent on the *Times'* letter pages noted that it was fortunate that the Lord Chancellor was proposing wide-ranging reforms to legal aid. 'Had he sought to merely paper over the cracks, this would have proved prohibitively expensive.'[6]

Access to justice

Lord Irvine's public profile noticeably diminished as the New Labour spin machine tried to keep him out of trouble. However, he was central to piloting through the changes in the legal aid system brought in under the Access to Justice Act 1999 and the Asylum and Immigration Act 1999.

In particular, the 'Access to Justice' legislation represented the biggest shake-up of legal aid since 1949. It replaced the LAB with the LSC, changed the rules on conditional fees, and introduced a hard cap on overall expenditure. The Act also established the Criminal Defence Service and includes a provision for salaried defenders; a controversial measure that had been taken out when the bill was in the House of Lords over concerns about the impartiality and independence of employed lawyers.

The most far-reaching change introduced by the Access to Justice Act was the cap on overall expenditure. Until this point, as discussed above, the LAB had largely controlled expenditure by altering scope and eligibility. The LAB had previously predicted expenditure and then lobbied the Treasury to fund increases when they went over budget. The change to a capped budget and a determination by the Treasury not to allow expenditure to exceed this was to have great significance in later years. It is perhaps the main reason behind the retrenching of civil legal aid in the second phase of New Labour.

Quality control

Franchising, or the quality mark system as it was to become known, was a continuation in policy from the previous Conservative regime under Lord McKay. LAG was a long-time supporter of franchising to address concerns over quality. On taking office, Irvine dusted off plans that had been drafted by civil servants under the Conservatives to make it compulsory to hold a specialist quality mark in order to apply for a block contract to undertake legal aid work. Restricting the Legal Help scheme (the contract for initial advice on matters which replaced the green form scheme) to contract holders would drastically reduce the number of firms offering legal aid. However, it would have the advantage of creating a level playing field in terms of quality and tackle the abuse of the green form scheme by some firms.

The Law Society opposed these changes. However, Chancery Lane's eye was off the ball as it was engulfed with its own internal difficulties. These had begun in 1995 with the election of Martin Mears as president on a platform of cutting back what he saw as an overly bureaucratic and unrepresentative organisation. His election split the Law Society's ruling council and there was much in-fighting. The organisation was hit by further problems after accusations of bullying by Law Society staff were made against vice president Kamlesh Bahl. Bahl eventually resigned in March 2000 and brought claims of racial and sexual discrimination against the Society.

There was also the Society's misconceived 'Justice Denied' campaign against the Access to Justice Bill. Full page advertisements in the national press were taken out featuring 'victims' of the government's legal aid cuts. The overtly political campaign brought Chancery Lane into damaging conflict with Irvine. He accused the advertisements of being 'a travesty of the facts' and the Society of 'propagating untruths'.[7]

Until early 2000, the Law Society was officially neutral on whether firms should apply for franchises. It was forced to come off the fence with the LAB's decision to make franchises compulsory for firms wanting to provide green form work, or Legal Help as it was to become, from January 2000. The Law Society Council agreed in September 1998 that all firms should apply for franchises. It remained opposed, though, to contracting. In response to the publication of the Access to Justice Bill, the Law Society argued that legal aid should not be restricted to contracted firms as this would reduce client choice.

There were divisions within the profession and a significant number of the larger criminal law firms split with Chancery Lane to carry out negotiations with the LAB over block contracting (which was the term in use at the time to describe contracts to carry out fixed amounts of legal aid work) and ultimately took part in a pilot. The LAB was also bypassing the Law Society and cultivating relationships directly with the larger firms in order to get feedback on policy changes because, according to Steve Orchard, 'due to the years of turmoil solicitors felt that they had no voice'.[8]

From January 2000, firms and not-for-profit agencies had to have a quality mark in the relevant area of law to be awarded a civil legal advice and assistance block contract. When the system came into force around 5,500 contracts were awarded to firms and organisations with franchises, including 50 out of 52 law centres. Citizens advice bureaux mainly received contracts in welfare benefits and debt. Robert Sayer, then president of the Law Society, accused legal aid reform of being introduced in 'a piecemeal and unco-ordinated manner'. 'Overnight, the number of firms offering initial advice to clients on legal aid will fall from 10,000 to 5,000 with the contracting system, but the public will not know how to find the remaining sources of help,' he said. 'The Lord Chancellor's Department is rushing into a grand experiment with the legal aid scheme – with the most vulnerable members of the public as its guinea pigs.' Contracting was the right policy to pursue in LAG's view, but it did reduce the number of suppliers thus reducing access points to the system for the public leading to further gaps.

South London legal aid practice Mackintosh Duncan launched a judicial review supported by the Law Society. Nicola Mackintosh, the firm's co-founder, said they were 'willing to do the work for our clients. We need to be supported by the LAB to do so, not prevented from providing our clients with the services they need. The board has a responsibility to ensure that vulnerable people have equal access to justice on the same footing as those able to pay for legal services. This scheme does exactly the opposite.' It was argued that the franchising scheme would have a detrimental impact on specialist firms, such as Mackintosh Duncan which specialised in mental health law, leading to clients being unable to receive the help they needed. The firm argued that there was a common law right of access to the courts and that people had a right to choose who represented them. Despite having some sympathy with these arguments, the court found that there was no absolute right to have access to the courts or for the state to provide money to pay for a lawyer.

Community Legal Service

The CLS was to be made up of a core of specialist quality-marked firms and not-for-profit agencies which overlapped with a much wider group of non-specialist services which were also to be quality-marked at information and advice levels. In attempting to integrate all civil general and legal advice services which had developed in parallel to the legal aid system into a seamless service the government was breaking new ground.

Five quality mark levels were eventually established for solicitor firms and other organisations: self-help information; assisted information; general help; general help with casework; and specialist help. Quality marks were also established for websites, telephone services and mediation services. A website, to provide information on legal matters and to signpost members of the public to providers, was also launched. The quality marks were essential to underpin an integrated system but were eventually to fall foul of the LSC's retrenchment, discussed below,

The success of the not-for-profit pilots which began under the previous government meant that Irvine was able to preside over a large-scale expansion of third sector involvement in the provision of civil legal aid, particularly those focused on giving specialist advice in social welfare law cases. This was one of the great successes of the CLS.

From taking government in 1997, the LAB and New Labour worked on putting the meat on the bare bones of the policy statement in the Labour manifesto committing the government to establishing the CLS. Thirteen regional committees were established in the first year of the new government to co-ordinate local planning of civil law services. Consisting of six members, four appointed from outside the LSC, they were asked to draw up plans for discrete geographical areas, which usually followed unitary local authority boundaries and became known as 'bid zones'. Using statistical data (including figures for means-tested benefits) they drew up plans for the provision of civil law services in their areas and prioritised the needs for new services. For example, the West Midlands Legal Services Committee found a high level of need for all areas of law in Birmingham, but low levels of need in the rural area of South Staffordshire.[9] This represented for the first time some rational planning in the system for providing civil legal aid services to the public. It was destined to be a short-lived phenomenon. Local planning was for a short period to be taken to a further level. In May 1999 the government published a consultation on the CLS in which it floated the idea of CLS partnerships in every bid zone to develop better local networks and to plan legal services. It was an idea that was soon to run out steam, not least because of a lack of resources.

Criminal Defence Service

The Criminal Defence Service (CDS) was a very different proposition in conception to the CLS. The new CDS mainly consisted of a repackaging of existing suppliers into a rebranded service under the criminal specialist quality mark, as well as integrating the budget for Crown and higher courts cases into the overall budget.

Firms were asked by the LSC to decide whether they wanted to become part of the new CDS by applying for advice and assistance work contracts including police station and magistrates' court work. These came into effect in April 2001. As with civil legal aid, quality marks were compulsory for firms wanting to undertake the work.

Before the launch of the CDS there were around 3,500 firms offering criminal law advice and assistance. The impact of the change was marginal – just over 500 firms dropped out, most undertaking small amounts of legal aid with little impact on clients.

In the run-up to the introduction of the CDS, the LSC was under pressure to make sure that enough firms signed up to the scheme to ensure it succeeded. There were protests by solicitors, including a threat of a 24-hour strike by some duty solicitors in November and a week of action in July 2000 organised by the Legal Aid Practitioners Group. In February 2001 a pay rise for criminal practitioners, the first in eight years, was offered at the last minute as a tactic to appear as a concession so that the Law Society would give a clear recommendation to firms to sign the new contracts. There were further concessions, including the continuation of payments under the old structure for police station work, to persuade the Law Society finally to recommend that firms sign the contracts.

Rearranging the deck chairs

This chapter covers the first phase of New Labour. Credit must be given to the government for trying to introduce a more rational system of planning and organisation to what had been largely haphazard in design. The major drawback to the CLS was that while it had created a bureaucracy which was identifying gaps in provision and raising quality standards, there was not the political will to find the cash to expand the service when need was identified.

In the teeth of opposition from providers, Lord Irvine had brought in major changes, taking personal injury cases out of scope and requiring all suppliers to be quality-marked in order to apply for contracts to provide legal aid services. He had also led the establishment of the CDS and the CLS. Behind that rebranding there was little of substance – apart from an attempt to knit together suppliers into a single service and the introduction of quality controls. The whole legal aid system was approaching crisis due to the most radical change brought in by the Access to Justice Act, the introduction of the hard cap on expenditure.

The introduction of compulsory specialist quality marks and block contracts did dramatically reduce the numbers of legal aid suppliers, particularly in civil legal aid. Despite the reduction in access points, the introduction of compulsory quality marks improved both advice and management standards. The quality mark generally benefited non-legal aid services as it impacted on the management of the whole organisation.

In what was to prove to be a final flourish for both Lord Irvine and Orchard, small increases in eligibility for civil legal aid were introduced in April and September 2002, as they both stepped down in June the following year. The April change brought a very modest 1.7 per cent of the population (around 150,000 people) into eligibility and in September the income cap above which people were not entitled to legal aid was raised from £2,034 per month to £2,250 for civil and family. This brought around 700,000 more people into eligibility. New Labour's new CLS was not a grand vision but more a pragmatic attempt to tie together existing resources into a coherent whole underpinned by the quality marks and more effective planning. While a few more people could claim legal aid (apart from the notable exception of immigration work, which had seen the extension of legal aid to representation in tribunals), in reality there were no additional funds for civil legal advice from the start of the CLS. For this reason, it is hard to see the introduction of the new service as much more than spin without substance. 'Rearranging the deck chairs on the Titanic', as one sceptic described it soon after its launch.[10]

1 *Report to the Lord Chancellor by Sir Peter Middleton*, September 1997.
2 Lord Woolf, *Access to justice – final report*, Lord Chancellor's Department, 1996, Ch 3.
3 *Further findings: A continuing evaluation of the civil justice reforms*, Department of Constitutional Affairs, August 2002.
4 *Independent* 23 January 1998.
5 *Times* 13 February 1998.
6 GMN Whiting to the *Times* 5 March 1998.
7 *Guardian* 29 April 1999.
8 LAG interview with Steve Orchard, May 2008.
9 *Assessment of need for legal service*, Report to the Legal Services Board 1998/99, West Midlands Legal Services Committee.
10 *Law Society Gazette* 6 April 2000.

CHAPTER 4

New Labour: from crisis to Carter

Political death is often sudden and unexpected, at least for the victim. On 11 June 2003 Lord Irvine visited newly established law centres in Manchester and attended a reception to celebrate their launch. He gave no hint that he was facing losing office the following day. By all accounts the details for his abrupt departure were not finalised until late that evening when he returned to London. His opposition to scrapping the role of Lord Chancellor played a part in Tony Blair's decision to dismiss his old mentor, as had the growing perception among New Labour ranks that he was a liability (whatever his merits as a reformer). As far as legal aid policy went, civil servants at the Legal Services Commission (LSC) and the Lord Chancellor's Department (LCD) had no idea that their boss was on his way out until it was announced.

There was change at the LSC as well when Steve Orchard, who had had a firm hand on the tiller of first the Legal Aid Board and then the LSC since 1989, announced his retirement at the end of June 2003. At that time, the legal aid budget was growing out of control in criminal and to a lesser extent in immigration – a reality acknowledged by Orchard as well as by politicians. In a parting interview, Orchard said that the biggest cost driver was criminal legal aid and this was being driven by government policy. Orchard and Irvine both fought to ringfence legal aid from the Treasury.

Charlie Falconer replaced Irvine as Lord Chancellor and swept into the LCD with radical plans to overhaul the department, not least to abolish his own job – or at least one of them. As a precursor to the scrapping of the role of Lord Chancellor, Falconer also occupied the newly created post of Secretary of State for Constitutional Affairs. On the day he was appointed, the new Department of Constitutional   47

Affairs was created with a remit, it said, 'to uphold justice, rights and democracy'.

In terms of personality, Falconer was the polar opposite of Irvine. Like his boss Tony Blair, Falconer had an outgoing personality, was charming and possessed good media skills. Also, like Blair, he cultivated an informal atmosphere around him encouraging officials and others to call him 'Charlie', a definite first for the ancient office of Lord Chancellor. The Lord Chief Justice, Lord Woolf, famously described Falconer as 'a cheeky chappie'. Whether a slight was intended or not, the condescending implication was that our esteemed Lord Chancellor was a bit of a lightweight.

A top rank lawyer, Falconer took silk in 1984 and built up a well remunerated commercial practice. He also had well-honed political skills, inheriting and surviving the perceived white elephant 'Millennium Dome' brief from Peter Mandelson, as well as chairing numerous cabinet committees, acting as an outrider for his close friend Blair. In contrast to Irvine, he proved himself a consummate media performer. Particularly in the latter days of the Blair government, Falconer would comment on a wide range of issues on behalf of the government while other cabinet members kept their heads down waiting for Gordon Brown's inauguration as premier.

Falconer knew Blair from school and, famously, they were flatmates together as young barristers. On taking power Blair had given his old friend a peerage and brought him into government. His close relationship with Blair meant he could push forward the planned reforms of the Lord Chancellor's responsibilities and office. At the same time it meant that it would be unlikely that Falconer would receive any favours from a Gordon Brown controlled treasury.

In 2001/02 the government published its spending plans for legal aid.[1] Over the next three years, it allowed for some modest growth in the overall budget:

20001/02: £1.717 billion (actual)
20002/03: £1.748 billion
20003/04: £1.819 billion
20004/05: £1.929 billion

The table in Appendix A provides a detailed breakdown of the figures for legal aid expenditure. That table reveals an overspend of £211.7 million by 2004/05. Big growth areas of expenditure were magistrates' court orders, high cost criminal cases and immigration cases. Richard Collins, until August 2008 the Executive Director for Policy at the LSC, described the increase in immigration expenditure as 'a toxic mix of the growth in asylum seekers and having to grow the supplier base of immigration practitioners'.[2] Chapter 7 describes in detail the reasons for the growth in criminal legal aid expenditure and the LSC's efforts to control it.

What is frequently glossed over in the debate on the cost of legal aid is the impact of bringing Crown Court and higher court cases into the budget. The headline-grabbing figure of £2 billion in expenditure on legal aid has been reached in large part by subsuming these cases into the overall budget and the growth in their cost. Prior to April 2003, legal aid for Crown and higher court cases had been administered by the courts. As can be seen from the table in Appendix A, by 2005/06 expenditure had grown to £695.5 million, which was almost one third (32.7 per cent) of the overall budget. In 2000/01, two years before being taken over by the LSC, the cost of Crown Court and higher court cases was £422 million, which would have been almost one quarter (24.3 per cent) of the overall budget.

Falconer was dogmatic in apportioning blame for the increase in high cost cases. 'Study any profession they will produce the system that gives them the most income. For example, if lawyers get money for the number of pages read, the number of pages read will go up.'[3] His explanation for the increasing costs of very high cost cases (that notorious category of cases that represented 1 per cent of total caseload but swallowed up almost 50 per cent of the Crown Court budget) in 1997/98 was that the Bar was 'using every part of the system to get as much as possible. Fees are still too high and cases are lasting too long. They are no more complicated than they were ten years ago'. Falconer might be correct, but the government's apparent blindness to other pressures on the criminal budget was of greater significance (see Chapter 7).

Falconer also argued that the introduction of the Legal Services Act 2007, which was passed after Sir David Clementi's review of regulation for legal services was an important part of 'breaking the hold of the lawyer on government' (rather like Lord Irvine 'facing down the vested interests').[4] Clementi's review led to the split of the legal professions into regulator and representative arms as well as establishing systems for independent oversight of complaints. The different legal practice structures introduced by the Act will lead to some freeing up of the market for legal services with opportunities for innovation in the provision of legal advice; however they could be outweighed by threats to High Street legal aid practice as firms will be forced to drop less remunerative parts of practice. The process of breaking down restrictive practices in the legal professions was well advanced prior to Falconer's term in office, for example, solicitors had lost their monopoly on conveyancing work under the previous Conservative government. The interests of legal aid clients have so far been largely overlooked in the debate around the future of legal services following the Legal Services Act (we return to this theme in Chapter 8).

The brewing crisis of spiralling legal aid costs saw commentators take a fairly despondent view of Falconer's Lord Chancellorship. As predicted by LAG in early 2003: 'Despite all the changes and upheaval of the Access to Justice Act 1999 and the introduction of contracts, we may be about to see the government return to using cuts in essential entitlements as a method of controlling the legal aid budget.'

Flagship policy sinks

Three years into the Community Legal Service (CLS), New Labour's flagship policy, the ministers commissioned a major review. Matrix Research and Consultancy was commissioned to undertake the review and reported in early 2004.[5] This report drew on evidence gathered from legal aid suppliers, local authorities and others involved in CLS partnerships. It clearly identified a number of fundamental weaknesses, not least a lack of clarity about the service's aims. It also recognised that it was vulnerable to policy changes in government and to the increasing cash demands of the Criminal Defence Service (CDS). The report was particularly damning on its central policy initiative – the CLS partnerships – through which it was hoped that the rather random state of local provision was to be co-ordinated for the first time. The Matrix report found their role unclear and any initial enthusiasm was already petering out due to lack of resources.

A fundamental problem, that the CLS proved itself not equipped to tackle, was the uneven spread of social welfare law services. The LSC was well aware of the problem. As was discussed in Chapter 2, legal aid supply has evolved on an ad hoc basis leading to different levels of provision. The table on page 68 shows the dramatically variable levels of spending across the country in social welfare law. Perversely, those councils which spend the most on social welfare law would have the most to lose if this or a future government decided to spread expenditure evenly across the country. The government's hope was that CLS partnerships would encourage the co-ordination and development of social welfare law services, but they were ineffectual for the reasons discussed in the next chapter. An obvious weakness was the lack of cash to develop services, making them an easy target for savings when the financial crisis hit.

The reality was that the Treasury took the view that expenditure on social welfare law was discretionary and could be axed to find savings to offset the increase in the cost of the CDS. To convince the Treasury not to cut expenditure the LSC embarked on its current strategy, described by Richard Collins, former head of policy at the LSC, as 'refocusing away from joining up services to increasing the numbers helped'. Local planning was abandoned to make cost savings while the LSC embarked on a strategy of encouraging greater numbers through the system to justify the expenditure. The final nail was driven into the coffin of local planning of legal aid services by the appointment of Sir Michael Bichard as head of the LSC in April 2005. Soon after joining he took the decision to kill off the regional planning committees. 'They were not delivering very much,' said Bichard. 'There was a moribund feel about the Commission with members spending 40% of their time in regional meetings which were of no benefit to providers or clients.'

At the end of 2008, in comparison to any other public services, most notably education and health, legal aid has no local dimension to the planning of services or consultation with the public on their expectations of the service. With the regional committees and CLS partnerships, public opinion – albeit mediated through suppliers – could be heard. Also, firms and the not-for-profit agencies had forums in which their views could be expressed.

Nonetheless, killing off the local planning structures was crucial in the cash-strapped world of legal aid to the next phase of the development of policy because it delivered some savings from a budget under pressure. The LSC consolidated power into a central London bureaucracy. Without the counter-balance of influence from the regions and local providers, it has been made easier for the LSC to disengage from suppliers' interests and pursue the strategy of becoming a 'procurement agency' rather than the administrator of the legal aid system.

Centralising the administration of the service also reflects the trend within government to take power away from local communities. Both Labour and Conservative governments at times have been strong on the rhetoric of local empowerment, but have often proved reluctant to devolve any real power. New Labour with its introduction of the Scottish Parliament, Welsh Assembly and London mayor bucked this trend in the early period of government, but has since returned to type.

Preferred supplier

In retrenching, the LSC also dropped its commitment to non-specialist quality marks as they were costly to provide audits for and were not relevant to the core business of administering the legal aid system. A new chief executive Clare Dodgson joined the LSC in June 2003. Early on in the post she signalled the LSC's intention to cut down the bureaucratic burden on suppliers.

The following year the LSC announced its preferred supplier pilots. The LSC wanted to adopt a 'lighter touch' on auditing and delegate more to suppliers. The system of quality audits which involved checking against check-lists of issues and procedures that should have been covered in a case as well as auditing an organisation's management systems was seen as cumbersome and expensive. Audits were unpopular with the profession who often complained that they were inexpertly conducted by poorly qualified staff and, on occasion, applied oppressively. That regime was to be replaced by peer review. The LSC had hoped to roll out its preferred supplier scheme nationally by 2006, but it was eventually abandoned in the aftermath of the Carter report. The LSC insisted that it had kept the 'key ingredients' of preferred supplier but it wanted responsibility for quality and accreditation to move to the Law Society as 'it should not be our business'. Much of the work could be outsourced with overall control in the hands of the Law Society, but there would need to be detailed negotiation around issues such as non-solicitor agencies and, from LAG's perspective, guarantees about the quality of service to the public.

The yo-yoing on policy initiatives between the Irvine and Falconer periods was divisive internally at the LSC. Tony Edwards, the LSC Commissioner responsible for the crime portfolio at that point, was disillusioned by the about-turn. 'Preferred supplier was one of the best things they've ever done and peer review, it could be groundbreaking and world-leading. It is deeply depressing to watch it being destroyed by what is going on now,' he said.

As well as dropping its plans for the introduction of the preferred supplier scheme, the LSC set the level for entering the system at 'threshold competence' – the lowest quality level. Firms and other suppliers might see this as cutting out unnecessary bureaucracy, but it represents a risk to quality, particularly with the introduction of fixed fees.

Breaking the stranglehold

The ministerial response to the perceived financial crisis in legal aid was the standard one. They commissioned a report. The Fundamental Legal Aid Review (FLAR) was announced by the minister with responsibility for legal aid, David Lammy, in May 2004. The review was intended to be a wide-ranging project which was to examine the root causes of the increases in expenditure in the system and to look at innovative ways of delivering the service in the future while giving value for money. Significantly, the Prime Minister's Strategy Unit provided assistance and departments including the Home Office and the Crown Prosecution Service were also consulted.[6]

No final report was published. It seems the report was buried as it did not reach conclusions that were politically acceptable. 'The FLAR produced nothing', said Falconer.[7] 'It did not come up with the fundamental change necessary. It did not address the issue of increasing costs of criminal legal aid ground into the system. Without this, [the criminal spend] would eventually end up taking the entire budget.'

The paper *A fairer deal for legal aid* published in July 2005 included a reference to the FLAR saying the paper sets out the conclusions of the review.[8] That paper provides the terms of reference for what was to become the Carter review. It was a classic piece of change management strategy. In the same way as an ailing business enacts some unpalatable restructuring to sell to a despondent workforce, the board brings in an outside management consultant to be the bearer of bad news.

It would seem that senior people within the LSC prior to Carter had made their minds up that the deployment of competitive tendering for criminal services was the solution to controlling costs. A pilot for the London region prior to the announcement of the Carter review was planned and fiercely opposed by suppliers. 'London competitive tendering was highly unpopular,' said Michael Bichard.[9] 'To have any chance of convincing people we needed an objective independent review as it was clear the profession was not going to accept competitive tendering.' One of Bichard's first discussions with Falconer on joining the LSC in April 2005 was who would be available to undertake such a review.

Again, it was time to take on those vested interests. 'It was my decision to get Lord Carter to undertake a review,' said Falconer in an interview for this book. He said he appointed Bichard 'as he could manage change'. 'We had to break the hold of the criminal practitioners and force them to restructure so we could get more control over the costs of provision.'

Get Carter

In ordering the Carter review, Falconer was following in the long line of reports and reviews to find the solutions that have beset legal aid since its inception. Falconer's main policy concern was the 37 per cent increase in criminal legal aid expenditure since Labour came to power and the 24 per cent decrease in civil (asylum excluded) and family legal aid. In establishing the Carter review his hope was that it would set in train the introduction of best value tendering (BVT) (the modified form of competitive tendering introduced by Labour when it came to power) which would lead to savings to boost spending on civil legal aid. He had no room for the expansion of the budget as the Treasury had set a ceiling of £2 billion on legal aid expenditure which is still current.

Falconer believes that from the mid-1980s the Treasury saw legal aid as a major item of expenditure and that the 'LCD was trying to keep the system alive ... as the state had discovered that legal aid was not subject to the same rigor of other areas of public expenditure'. Prior to Falconer arriving at the LCD, he reckons that there was 'a real determination by the Treasury that the Department should keep to its DEL (Departmental Expenditure Limit)'.

Change was being foisted on the LSC whether the organisation liked it or not. On the civil side of the LSC, policy was developed in parallel to the ongoing Carter review. A July 2005 consultation paper outlining a draft strategy was largely welcomed by commentators as it tried to address the issue of better co-ordinating services so that they were more able to tackle the clusters of problems clients face. For example, a person dismissed from his or her job might have a potential unfair dismissal claim, plus benefits and debt problems. However, controversially, the paper proposed the provision of joint tenders with local authorities for social welfare and family law services – Community Legal Advice Centres or CLACs as they became known. To justify the policy the LSC drew on the *Causes of Action* paper published by the Legal Services Research Centre.[11] While the research does support the contention that clients face clusters of problems, it is based on a survey of the general population and not the group eligible for legal aid.

Lord Carter published his report in July 2006.[11] Its main recommendations were:

Criminal

- redrawing duty solicitor schemes into larger boundaries and introducing block contracts for police station work;
- fixed fees for police station work;
- graduated fee scheme for magistrates' court work;
- reform fees paid in Crown Court cases;
- panels to bid for high cost cases on a BVT basis; and
- a spending cut of 20 per cent in Crown Court cases and a rebalancing of work away from the senior to junior bar.

Civil

- fixed or graduated fees for all work;
- a 'unified' contract for all civil work and limiting contracts to either £25,000 or £50,000; and
- BVT to be introduced for all civil contracts with suppliers bidding against criteria including quality.

Carter acknowledged in the report that some organisations would have to merge or discontinue legal aid work as the market consolidated. He argued that the transition to competitive tendering must be managed carefully.

The intellectual case for competitive tendering has never been persuasive. There is evidence from the experience of contracting for criminal legal aid services in North America to indicate that there are reductions in quality and the creation of cartels which lead to an increase in costs. For example, in San Diego criminal defence service costs rose by 65 per cent after the introduction of competitive bidding.[12] The American Bar Association has also highlighted the increases in prices and concerns over quality, which have followed the introduction of competitive tendering.

Much of government and LSC thinking on the costs of criminal legal aid assume that lawyers are to blame. Professors Ed Cape and Richard Moorhead undertook research on the cost drivers in criminal defence work. They concluded that 'decisions taken beyond the remit and direct influence of the LSC and of defence lawyers have had a significant effect on criminal legal expenditure, and account for a significant proportion of the increase in expenditure over the last decade'.[13] 'The Ministry of Justice are no nearer getting to grips with the causes of why criminal legal aid expenditure has grown', concluded Cape. The academic did offer some pointers as to likely factors. 'The greater use of imprisonment will lead to more expenditure on criminal legal aid as the likelihood of loss of liberty is the most common reason for the grant of legal aid. We are also seeing the numbers of arrests creeping up and these result in a greater need for advice.'

Fixing costs

In preparation for the introduction of BVT, the LSC introduced a system of fixed fees for all civil and criminal legal aid work. A new contract was also introduced for suppliers which did away with the two different types of payment. Prior to this most not-for-profit suppliers received a fixed payment for a block of work while the private practice solicitors were paid by the case. Transitional arrangements were put in place for the not-for-profit suppliers.

The LSC originally wanted to introduce the contracts and fixed fees in April 2007, but postponed the introduction to later in the year after pressure from the Ministry of Justice and suppliers. This meant that the reforms were undertaken in two stages.

The first stage of introducing the unified contracts and then the fixed fees went ahead. Solicitors threatened to boycott the introduction of the contracts. Legal aid lawyers had long been frustrated by the Law Society and its perceived lack of willingness to take on ministers over legal aid policy. However, Desmond Hudson's arrival in September 2006 apparently sharpened Chancery Lane's campaigning zeal. In March 2007 a poll of law firms by the Law Society showed that 58 per cent were considering not signing it. The Law Society also issued advice from its legal advisers not to sign. 'It is unfathomable that the government is still pushing ahead with these perilous reforms in their current form,' said Desmond Hudson. 'It must stop being so cavalier about the risks to the legal aid system and reconsider the so-called reforms before it's too late.' The Constitution Reform Committee led by Liberal Democrat Alan Beith damned the proposals as 'a breathtaking risk'.[14]

The Law Society won a reprieve for the profession on the introduction of fixed fees in criminal legal aid following a judicial review. This threw the LSC into disarray. It eventually decided to give notice of termination on the existing criminal contracts and re-tender them to start from January 2008. For some firms this was the last straw. Fisher Meredith, the large South London firm, decided that it no longer wished to undertake criminal legal aid work. They reckoned that the fixed fees would mean a 9 per cent reduction in pay for police station work and a 16 per cent reduction in fees for magistrates' court work.

While the LSC denies it, it was concerned that large numbers of solicitors would refuse to sign the new contracts for the April 2007 deadline. In the second showdown of the New Labour period, the first being the introduction of compulsory contracts, both sides played a game of brinkmanship over contracts, but again the firms cracked and signed in large numbers. The LSC later said in its annual report that 95 per cent of private practice firms signed the contract.

Law centres also backed boycotting the contract at their 2006 conference. Richard Jenner, director of the Advice Services Alliance, said that those not-for-profit agencies that were geared 'towards doing many straightforward cases [would] be fine. Our concern is those agencies that undertake complex cases and/or cases for clients with language difficulties, disabilities or other special needs are going to struggle'. LAG believes that Jenner is correct. Law centres face just such a difficulty, for example Stockport Law Centre closed in November 2007 citing the pressure from the change to fixed fees.

Carter delayed

At the time of going to press in early 2009, the reform programme has hit major problems. Any momentum appears to have dissipated, mainly because the big expenditure item – Crown Court and other higher court work – has proved impossible to tackle.

We are at a crossroads. In LAG's view the Carter vision was simply wrong. It was predicated on an overly simplistic belief in 'the market' being able to sort out the problem. But there was a failure to understand what 'the problem' was, that the publicly-funded legal sector has evolved in a complex and haphazard fashion and is one that will not withstand shocks. Putting all that aside, the implementation of the Carter review is proving a hugely botched job. The blueprint for reform has had to be compromised by a revolt from the profession and endless finessing by the LSC.

Despite 2,300 individual barristers joining the specialist criminal panel, only 130 agreed to the new contracts on offer in March 2008. This led to a standoff with the Bar. The Bar eventually negotiated a compromise with the Ministry of Justice and the LSC. This meant an increase in fees for very high cost cases of 5 per cent at a cost of £6 million (paid for by reducing the number of cases in which two barristers can be instructed) to July 2009 and thereafter a revised payment scheme based on graduated fees.

The Law Society won a second judicial review in November 2007 on the legality of the civil legal aid contract. That ruling led to a welcome ceasefire between the LSC and the profession and a three-way deal between the Ministry of Justice, the LSC and Chancery Lane. The main points were no price-competitive tendering until 2013; some small increases in the rates paid in cases; a closed list of community legal advice centres and networks for the period ending April 2010; and a delay on BVT until July 2009. Carolyn Regan, chief executive of the LSC, has described the agreement as heralding a 'genuinely different relationship with the Law Society as we now have five years of stability'.

New Labour's desire (in the words of Lord Irvine) to 'face down the vested interests' has often, but not always, betrayed a lack of understanding and appreciation of publicly-funded law. Forcing change on a profession of people – many of whom (not all) undertake a poorly remunerated area of the law out of a commitment to helping the vulnerable – has proved impossible. The former LSC chair Michael Bichard has been sanguine about the judicial review decisions, telling LAG that he told ministers that it was 'inevitable when introducing these changes that they might at some stage lose a judicial review', a comment that suggested a tendency towards bravado on the part of the LSC during this latter part of the New Labour period. A combination of legal challenges, the pressures within the LSC as a result of its struggles to control the budget and the need to cut back on its administrative budget by 30 per cent have caused delays in the reform programme.

There seems to be confusion as to what the reforms are trying to achieve. For example, in July 2008 at LSC's press conference to announce its response to the consultation on BVT of criminal defence services, chief executive Carolyn Regan conceded that it was 'never the intention with BVT to save money'. If that is the case, it seems legitimate to ask why policy makers are intent on putting the system through the pain of major restructuring.

BVT will not now be introduced for criminal legal aid until 2011 and for civil legal aid it has been put back to 2013. At the time of writing the budget is on target through a combination of changes in scope and the introduction of fixed fees to deliver savings.

1 LSC annual report 2000/01.
2 LAG interview with Richard Collins, June 2008.
3 LAG interview with Lord Falconer, July 2008.

4   Sir David Clementi, *Report of the Review of the Regulatory Framework for Legal Services in England and Wales,* December 2004.

5   Department for Constitutional Affairs, *The Independent Review of the Community Legal Service,* April 2004.

6   DCA news release, 17 May 2004.

7   LAG interview with Lord Falconer, July 2008.

8   *A fairer deal for legal aid* Cm 6591, TSO, 2005.

9   LAG interview with Sir Michael Bichard, June 2008.

10   Pascoe Pleasence et al, *Causes of action: civil law and social justice. The final report of the first LSRC survey of justiciable problems,* LSC, 2004.

11   *Legal aid: a market-based approach to reform,* July 2006.

12   Roger Smith, *Legal aid contracting,* LAG, 1998.

13   Ed Cape and Richard Moorhead, *Demand induced supply? Identifying cost drivers in criminal defence work. A report to the Legal Services Commission,* Legal Services Research Centre, July 2007.

14   *Implementation of the Carter Review of Legal Aid* HC 223-1, 2007, para 20.

CHAPTER 5

The CLS: mind the gap

During the course of 2006 a 62-year-old man regularly travelled between his Merthyr Tydfil home and his lawyer in West London. The man had a cottage on a farm in South Wales and his farmer-landlord was attempting to evict him. The man felt compelled to make the journey by bus, train and tube because a Kensington-based solicitor was the closest legal aid lawyer he could find. 'The first thing that we would do was give him something to eat and a cup of tea because he would never have enough money for food,' recalled Russell Conway, a partner at West London firm Oliver Fisher solicitors.[1] The solicitor saw the man half a dozen times over the course of six months before his client was able to transfer his case to a solicitor in Bristol.

New Labour's manifesto commitment for a Community Legal Service (CLS) was to provide the public with a 'comprehensive' network of legal support matching local demand with available provision.[2] This was expressed clearly in the 1998 paper *Modernising justice* which said that the CLS would 'ensure that every community has access to a comprehensive network of legal service providers of consistently good quality, so that people with actual or potential legal problems are able to find the information and help they need'.[3]

Such a commitment was always going to be tough to deliver, not least because of the fragmented and disparate nature of providers. The increasing economic pressures on mixed economy private practice law firms meant many abandoned legal aid, while the vagaries of the funding arrangements for not-for-profit advice agencies contributed to an uneven and changing landscape of provision.

The CLS has provided threadbare cover, and the pressures currently on the system means that it could unravel alarmingly. From the start of the CLS, the immediate concern expressed by LAG was of a growing legal aid 'desertification' as gaps appeared to open up in parts of the country. The existence of such 'deserts' has always proved hard to measure and prompted controversial claims from both practitioners and the government.

The disagreement between practitioners at the sharp end and the LSC as to the extent of gaps in provision has been unhelpful. It has also highlighted a major failure in the system. The LSC has repeatedly dismissed practitioner concerns as anecdotal, arguing that these gaps in provision were merely local problems rather than signs of a systematic undermining of publicly-funded law. In case of the man from Merthyr Tydfil, the LSC insisted that there were '45 specialist housing legal aid suppliers within 40 miles of Merthyr Tydfil' at the time. That assertion was countered convincingly by practitioners and the Law Society. In that instance, as is often the case, phone advice was not appropriate because the case involved a consideration of detailed plans, photographs and documents. Whatever the reality of availability of advice, the man (who faced the demolition of his home of 50 years) felt compelled to make the trip.

'Coverage' had long been an issue when it came to the provision of civil legal aid. But the gaps ironically became particularly marked after the creation of the CLS. In 2003 the Law Society claimed that for a tenant living in Kent who faced eviction at the hands of a dodgy landlord but could not afford legal advice, his or her nearest solicitor was either in Sussex or London. It also reckoned there were only a handful of divorce lawyers serving central London and only one criminal defence lawyer in Cambridgeshire covering a population of 50,000. In the same year an Essex woman tried to find legal advice on the finances of her divorce. 'I called more than 20 London solicitors, only to find that not one of them took legally aided divorce any more,' she said.[4]

The introduction of the CLS kickstarted a necessary debate about what we, as a society, should expect from publicly-funded civil law. Eligibility for civil legal aid has been slashed to the level of poverty benefit tied to eligibility for means-tested welfare benefits. If eligibility levels in civil legal aid continue to be reduced at the rate that they have been under New Labour, then the service is heading for extinction well within a decade. There are questions that need to be asked of policy-makers. Is the CLS a largely reactive service responding to people's needs as in the Legal Aid Board (LAB) model or is it about the commissioning of legal services targeting social exclusion as the LSC now suggests? If it is the latter, it needs to be properly resourced. An independent review of the CLS in 2004 concluded that there was a need to clarify its role in 'fighting social exclusion'. That lack of a coherent sense of identity has yet to be resolved. The same review concluded that what was 'specifically lacking' was 'an evidence base' linking the provision of publicly funded legal advice and achieving that end. 'The evidence indicated that there was a belief that reducing social exclusion was not part of the strategy for the CLS or had only recently become an aim of the CLS,' it said. Apparently the 'stakeholders seemed surprised that the CLS was about "fighting social exclusion" at all'. Does a private practice solicitor embark upon a career in the law to fight social exclusion? Probably not. However an adviser at a citizens' advice bureau might see his or her job in those terms.

'Ad hoc, unplanned and unco-ordinated'

The ambitions for a CLS were laudable. Policy-makers had long wanted to inject coherence and structure into a disparate and fragmented advice sector. 'There are many existing information and advice sources: the CABx, the law centres, the advice centres, and mediation bodies. We intend to co-ordinate these services under a coherent scheme which will provide a service to the whole public which is both easy to access and to understand,' said the Lord Chancellor, Lord Irvine, at the 1997 Law Society conference in Cardiff.

According to a consultation paper published in May 1999 many people received effective legal help, but 'if you live in an area with few or no convenient advice centres, or do not know where to go for help, you can end up having to work very hard to find support, travelling a long distance, or receiving no support to all'.[5] That paper attempted to describe a sprawling advice sector comprising private practice lawyers, independent advice centres, citizens' advice bureaux and law centres. 'This effort is on a scale without rival anywhere in the world and a great tribute to the community spirit of our people,' it said. 'It involves nearly 6,000 professional staff and some 30,000 unpaid volunteers working in over 3,000 centres, dealing with over 10 million inquiries each year. Total public funding is difficult to estimate accurately but probably £250 million a year. On the face of it, this provision should be adequate to meet priority need.' As the paper went on to demonstrate, this provision might have been testimony to great commitment, but it was also a chaotic way to provide a public service. It stated:

Despite the fact that nearly 2,000 separate agencies are involved, a person may be unable to find the right kind of help for his or her particular problem, within a reasonable distance of home, because:

- services have grown up in an *ad hoc*, unplanned and unco-ordinated manner dependent on discretionary funding from local authorities, charities and central government;
- need is not assessed coherently, as funding for advice is provided by a range of separate bodies without any co-ordination or common systems;
- as a result funding does not consistently follow need and those running agencies find that far too much of their time is spent dealing with various separate funders who each have their own criteria for funding;
- there is no common database advice providers on which people can draw, nor any standard quality accreditation system of which they can rely;
- cross-referrals and networking does not always occur.

Three major strands to the new CLS emerged. It would be a 'comprehensive' service; based on 'an effective assessment of local needs'; and with quality standards achieved through kite marks.

The service as envisaged by the Access to Justice Act 1999 covered the provision of basic information about the law as well as legal services, help preventing or resolving disputes and enforcing decisions, and other services such as mediation in family or civil cases. The scheme would cover advice, assistance and representation by both lawyers and non-lawyers through the new contracting regime or through employing staff to provide services directly to the public. Its ambition was to provide a network of service providers having to meet recognised quality standards using existing networks supported by newly co-ordinated funding based on an assessment of local needs.

The CLS was to build on existing policy initiatives predating New Labour, such as contracting which had provided for the first time a mechanism through which the LAB (and then the LSC) could target public funds regionally and according to legal advice type. In tandem with the roll-out of contracting, the LAB had begun to develop statistical needs assessment models and regional legal services committees to plan local strategy.

The Access to Justice Act introduced the CLS quality mark accreditation scheme. Providers would display the quality mark to show that they met the standard required. This built on franchising and the Legal Aid Franchise Quality Assurance Standard (LAFQAS). Under the CLS, it was compulsory to have the quality mark. Voluntary compliance had contributed to more than one-third (38 per cent) of suppliers delivering over two-thirds (68 per cent) of legally-aided work submitting to the franchising quality requirements in return for better rates of pay.[6] Compulsion under the new CLS was to strip out some 6,000 legal aid providers; most of them were small and many were 'dabblers'.

The CLS also introduced the CLS partnerships, representing the interests of both funders and providers of local legal services. They marked the first national initiative to co-ordinate services (previously funding of advice had evolved in a largely ad hoc manner). The idea was that this would be the mechanism for joining up the disparate sources of legal advice. Funders included the relevant office of the LSC, local authorities and other bodies, and providers included solicitors, citizens advice bureaux, advice agencies, law centres and housing aid centres. The idea behind the CLS partnerships was to identify the local level of need for legal services and evaluate the extent to which those needs were met by existing providers. 'This information enables each of the organisations participating in the partnership to decide what action they can take (as funders or as providers) to match provision better to local needs,' the LSC explained. 'The action may be taken by a single organisation or by several partners working together.'[7]

Other proposals were for a website (called *Just Ask*) so the public could access online legal information and co-ordinate other useful websites, and a CLS directory providing information on local solicitors, legal advice and information services in England and Wales. As far as buildings blocks go – CLS partnerships, a directory plus a website – this seemed an insubstantial foundation for what was pitched as the creation of a new service.

The success of the CLS

An independent review by Matrix Research and Consulting of the CLS in 2004 found that there was an ideological hole at its centre.

> This has meant that the agenda for the CLS is not sufficiently clear. The review has illustrated that there is a need to define the role and strategy for the CLS, clarifying its role in tackling social exclusion and establishing performance management systems to enable delivery.[8]

In particular, the Matrix report identified that there was no evidence base to support the extent to which advice and legal services 'contribute to the reduction of social exclusion'. Matrix also revealed a leadership vacuum, arguing that there was a 'lack of overall accountability for the CLS and no clear dedicated leader driving change'. The report also called for the CLS budget to be protected from the rising costs of criminal legal services and claimed that the contracting and quality assurance regimes were 'seemingly overly complex, burdensome, costly and bureaucratic'.

CLS partnerships, the cornerstone of the new service, were identified as already failing. Matrix also flatly observed that the CLS needed to 'develop means through which the aims of the CLS are reflected in local provision of information and advice'. It was hard to object to the ambition behind CLS partnerships, but it was easy to foresee that a lack of common interest – both between funders and providers and between providers themselves – would mean the initiative would prove a frustrating endeavour.

By March 2003 the LSC claimed that CLS partnerships had achieved over 99 per cent coverage of the population in England and Wales. There was little enthusiasm from providers, particularly private practice, as there was little by way of financial resource to support the partnerships themselves and no resources allocated to spend once provision gaps had been identified, apart from £5 million available through the Partnership Innovation Budget. Adam Griffith, policy officer at the Advice Services Alliance, articulated this tension in June 2003. 'My worry is that the CLSPs will increasingly be asked to make decisions about priorities and the rationing of existing resources,' he said. 'This could pit funders against providers and providers against each other and threaten any sense of trust and partnership which has been developed.'

That seemed to be the conclusion of a research project by the same group in 2004 which found that many CLS partnerships were already 'dormant or dying on their feet'.[9] Most of the 20 respondents questioned by researchers 'thought that their CLSPs had done nothing to meet the needs identified by the partnerships and had failed to make a difference'. Consequently, they were being deserted by private practice solicitors and community groups and were failing to engage funders other than local authorities and the LSC. 'Almost by tacit agreement the partnership has ceased to meet. I think everybody has just sort of said: "Well thank God that has died",' said one practitioner. Another said: 'There generally seems to be quite an air of disillusionment about, you know, "is there any point in actually going to these meetings any more?".' The malaise was confirmed in Citizens Advice's research which found that bureaux were active participants in partnerships (93 per cent of respondent bureaux were involved) but only 16 per cent felt that their efforts were justified.[10] CLS partnerships' fate was sealed. At their height, they were employing 130 staff to undertake the work. 'It made no sense at a time when there were falling numbers getting legal help to spend all our time joining up services,' said Richard Collins in 2008, then head of policy at the LSC.[11] 'Our view was that regional planning and partnership were not delivering.'

Ministers were also keen to develop the 'brand' of the CLS to assist the public to identify sources of legal help and guide them through the maze of advice providers. The familiar and immediately identifiable legal aid 'picnic table' was scrapped in favour of a new logo – described by the legal commentator Marcel Berlins as looking like Isadora Duncan's scarf 'just before it was caught in the wheels of a car and strangled her'. A number of CLS 'champions' – such as 'That's Life' presenter Esther Rantzen and Jenni Murray from Radio 4's 'Woman's Hour' – were appointed. Beyond the initial photo opportunities, no clear media strategy was discernible. Almost eight years after the launch, the CLS has almost zero public recognition. The failed attempt at rebranding was underscored by a misguided attempt to rename 'legal aid', a term that was familiar to most if not all, as 'CLS funding'. It seems that even the LSC has reinstated 'legal aid' in its communications, although this is not yet official policy.

Mind the gap

Access to justice quickly became the issue under the CLS. As said at the start of the chapter, the evidence as to provision gaps has been largely subjective and anecdotal. According to Citizens Advice in 2004 more than one in three bureaux (39 per cent) considered themselves to be in an 'advice desert'; over two-thirds (68 per cent) reported difficulties finding solicitors to take on immigration cases; around one-third had problems for family law (58 per cent) and housing (60 per cent). 'Overall the CLS scheme has brought improvements, such as the quality mark and new methods of delivering pilots, which may not have been achieved under the legal aid system,' the paper argued. 'However it is impossible to ignore evidence that growing numbers of solicitors firms are finding the contracting regime unworkable and pulling out.' The report referenced Law Society research which found since August 2002 a 12 per cent reduction in the number of firms offering legally-aided services following the introduction of the CLS

A 2006 Law Centre Federation survey also illustrated how its members were struggling to keep up with demand. Avon and Bristol Law Centre had 2,103 enquiries relating to immigration at its reception in the previous year; 908 relating to employment; 418 relating to housing; and 228 to debt. Its advisers provided advice and assistance in 399 immigration cases; 236 employment cases; 67 housing cases; and 28 debt cases. That research suggested that areas of the increasingly threadbare fabric of the CLS were being pushed beyond endurance. Victoria McNally of Brent Community Law Centre in north London reported a disturbing trend of users' frustration being directed towards staff members. She described all their cases as 'urgent' and requiring 'immediate action'. 'The first time in our 35 year existence, a member of staff was assaulted and knocked unconscious. This is symptomatic of an increased climate of clients being blocked from the system and becoming increasingly desperate.'[12]

The unevenness of legal aid provision across the country was starkly illustrated in 2008 as a result of a Freedom of Information Act request by the Advice Services Alliance.

Regional legal aid spend

Top five spenders	LSC indicative	Actual spend	% spend against indicative
Camden	£590,983	£2,206,712	373.4
Hackney and City	£663,945	£2,209,640	332.8
Tower Hamlets	£639,317	£1,689,447	264.26
Ealing	£641,831	£1,579,569	246.1
Liverpool	£1,187,302	£2,798,663	235.72
Bottom five spenders			
Surrey	£2,264,806	£529,271	23.37
East Riding	£710,950	£529,271	26.91
Kingston	£632,527	£173,065	27.36
South Hertfordshire	£1,396,982	£425,061	30.43
Bexley	£407,806	£144,457	35.42

The LSC had developed a formula for calculating the allocation of spending between different geographical areas allowing for variation of 15 per cent from its own estimates (see spend against indicative table). Some London boroughs are spending more than three times what the LSC calculated should be spent whereas others, such as Kingston and Bexley, were receiving less than half of what they should. Outside London, the LSC reckoned that areas like Liverpool, Middlesbrough and North Tyneside are spending more than twice what they should be.

The CLS mark 2

Five years into the CLS, and the LSC was looking to redesign fundamentally the service through a different initiative known as the Community Legal Advice Centres (CLACs) securing local provision in terms of both coverage and advice category. It was a radical departure with the LSC planning to take a more centralist role in controlling how advice was provided and who would provide it. In the wake of the Matrix review, former law centre manager Crispin Passmore was made the first director of the CLS four years after it was launched. The idea was to have 'jointly funded, face-to-face legal and advice services' to specialise in social welfare law and combine disparate services in a one-stop shop. Community Legal Advice Networks (CLANs) would exist in rural areas where communities were too disparate to make a CLAC work.

At the time of going to press, the CLAC initiative is being rolled out. It should be seen in light of a significant realignment of the provider base, especially in social welfare law, away from private practice to the not-for-profit sector. New Labour has been increasingly keen to involve the third sector in all parts of policy and this was made explicit in the CLS. In 2002 the LSC was set a target of providing £20 million of contracted work through not-for-profit agencies. Under Passmore's directorship, each year the LSC has improved on that figure and in 2007/08 more than £80 million was spent through the not-for-profit sector. Such contracts accounted for 31 per cent of its annual Legal Help expenditure and 67 per cent of its provision of social welfare law.[13]

The CLAC initiative has been significantly informed by the work of the Legal Services Research Centre in its paper, *Causes of action*.[14] The paper, which claimed to be the most in-depth and long-term study into civil justice problems, highlighted the phenomenon of 'problem clusters' where problems are experienced simultaneously or in sequence by the same person. The report identified 'three principal and distinct problem clusters' – family (domestic violence, divorce, relationship and children problems); homelessness (rented housing, homelessness and benefits); and economic (money and debt, consumer, and employment problems). The research also emphasised the knock-on consequences on the public purse of legal problems. It found that one-third of civil law problems affected people's health (18 per cent of problems led to stress-related ill health and 16 per cent led to physical ill health) and four out of five needed medical treatment. The LSC concluded that the research was evidence of 'the importance of joined up public services' and 'our new strategy for the CLS will make a real difference in tackling these challenges'.

The conclusion by the policy-makers was that the public needed co-ordinated advice, ideally one-stop-shops to avoid them being passed from pillar to post or simply lost in the system. 'There is now a widely held acceptance that seamless and integrated services are vital if we are to meet the legal advice needs of the most excluded clients,' wrote Crispin Passmore, director of the CLS in 2006, referencing *Causes of action*. In that year only six legal aid providers in the whole of England and Wales delivered specialist legal aid services in all five social welfare law categories – community care, debt, employment, housing and welfare benefits. No law centres had that coverage and only half of the 470 citizens advice bureaux undertook specialist legal advice at all.

Justice for the few ...

One of the most striking trends about access to justice under the CLS is the alarming shrinking of eligibility. 'People need to have ways to uphold their rights and defend their interests ... it is not enough for people to have rights, they must be confident they can enforce those rights if need be,' wrote Lord Irvine in his foreword to *Modernising justice*. This reflected the original aim for civil legal aid in the Legal Aid and Advice Act 1949 – 'no one will be financially unable to prosecute a just and reasonable claim or defend a legal right'.

That ambition has been eroded significantly. When the legal aid scheme was conceived by the Attlee government, around 80 per cent of the population was going to be eligible. In 1986 it was reckoned that almost two-thirds of the population was eligible (63 per cent), that dropped to 50 per cent by 2000 and then to less than one in three (29 per cent) in 2007 (see table).

Legal Aid Eligibility

Year	Estimated proportion of the population of England and Wales eligible for civil representation
1998	52%
1999	51%
2000	50%
2001	46%
2005	41%
2007	29%

According to the Ministry of Justice and the LSC, the drop in eligibility is the result of a number of factors: an increase in average earnings faster than the rate of inflation, demographic changes relating to age and partnership status of the population, the introduction of working tax credits and child tax credits as well as reforms to civil legal aid. It is argued that the reduction in eligibility is not down to a reduction in passportable benefits. Although claimants of income support and income-based jobseeker's allowance have until 2008 declined, the introduction of pension credit in 2003 has significantly increased the size of the passported population.

It was Pascoe Pleasence's *Causes of action* research that most recently mapped the reported incidences of the different types of civil legal problems. This research drew on the *English and Welsh Civil and Social Justice Survey* of over 5,000 respondents conducted in 2001 and 2004. It was consumer problems that were reported most frequently (13 per cent in 2001 and 10 per cent in 2004) and immigration and nationality issues least frequently (one-third of 1 per cent in 2001 and one-fifth of 1 per cent in 2004).

The research also found that for almost one in five problems (19 per cent) reported, no action was taken. As the research says, this indicates 'a profound need for knowledge ... about obligations, rights, remedies, and procedures for resolving justiciable problems'. The 2004 Matrix review of the CLS showed that the introduction of contracting and greater control of expenditure was doing little in the battle against social exclusion. The research did reveal 'a marked shift in expenditure patterns away from civil representation (ie, court cases) and towards legal help (ie advice and assistance)'. That was explained 'in part at least' by the removal of personal injury from

Reported incidence of problem types

Problem type	2001 N	2001 %	2004 N	2004 %
Consumer	748	13.3	503	10.0
Neighbours	471	8.4	329	6.6
Money/debt	465	8.3	279	5.6
Employment	344	6.1	260	5.2
Personal injury	217	3.9	244	4.9
Rented housing	215	3.8	137	2.7
Owned housing	135	2.4	121	2.4
Welfare benefits	127	2.3	98	1.9
Relationship breakdown	124	2.2	84	1.7
Divorce	122	2.2	106	2.1
Children	108	1.9	75	1.5
Clinical negligence	92	1.6	79	1.6
Domestic violence	88	1.6	42	0.8
Discrimination	80	1.4	111	2.2
Unfair treatment by the police	38	0.7	40	0.8
Homelessness	36	0.6	61	1.2
Mental health	26	0.5	11	0.2
Immigration	18	0.3	16	0.3

the legal aid scheme, but 'it may also be evidence of a shift towards greater funding for areas of social welfare law more strongly associated with the fight against exclusion'. However, Matrix found that there had been increases in contracts for certain areas of law (public law, community care, actions against the police, education, immigration, clinical negligence and mental health) and reductions in others (such as family, welfare benefits, housing, debt, employment and consumer). 'As welfare benefits, debt and housing are numerically the most significant and are most closely associated with social exclusion, the overall picture does not support the view that contracting has refocused LSC funding by directing it towards social exclusion,' it noted.

The LSC breaks down civil legal aid into 14 categories – the two big groups are family (see Chapter 6) and social welfare law which comprises the five categories of community care, debt, employment, housing and welfare benefits. Of those categories, the big three are debt, welfare benefits and housing. In 2000/01 there were 56,116 completed matters in debt which has gradually risen to 111,708 in 2007/08 (18,514 matters were dealt with by advisers on the Community Legal Advice (CLA) helpline). There were 101,525 completed matters in welfare benefits in 2000/01 (dipping to 78,046 in 04/05 due in part to the ending of the green form scheme) rising to 120,028 in 2007/08 (15,226 matters dealt with on the CLA helpline). In housing there were 106,735 completed matters in 2000/01 rising to 159,118 in 2007/08 (which includes 20,558 on the CLA helpline plus 30,472 through court duty schemes). The number of certificates in housing work has been relatively stable – around 12,000 a year. By contrast, the other two categories are small – in employment, 14,013 completed matters in 2000/01 and 21,076 in 2007/08 (including 9,527 through the CLA helpline) and in community care, 2,392 in 2000/01 and 4,680 in 2007/08 (see Appendix 2).

In 2007/08, 250,877 members of the public were helped by the CLA helpline (formerly CLS Direct which began in July 2006 and in 2005/06 assisted 75,000 people).[15] The first 15 minutes of advice are provided non-means-tested by a generalist adviser and thereafter callers have to be eligible.

The LSC has been putting considerable resources into its new telephone advice service. Although the number of callers fell in 2007/08, mainly as a result of the introduction of an operator service to screen calls, the telephone service reaches those members of the public who would otherwise never enter a citizens advice bureau, let alone a solicitor's office. The helpline, though, can be no replacement for face-to-face services. There are also concerns about the quality of advice and its usefulness for callers. A rough and ready 'mystery shopper' in 2006 conducted by a panel of experts produced variable results.[16] At the time, Lambeth County Court was routinely stamping all envelopes containing claims forms for tenants in possession cases with CLS Direct's 0845 number. Out of ten calls made and analysed, six prompted detailed responses, and in four of those cases experts detected further advice was needed. In two cases, callers were prevented from taking appropriate legal action. 'In principle, CLS Direct should be a good vehicle for building support for legal aid,' said

Roger Smith, former LAG director and one of the experts. He was concerned that advisers seemed reluctant to refer callers on for face-to-face help. 'On this snapshot, the advice seems somewhat variable. A potential weakness was always likely to be appropriate "referral after" advice. If this scheme works, some callers will be satisfied by their call, but others should be encouraged to take matters further.' The LSC has to make sure that CLS Direct 'isn't just a mechanism for deterring demand,' Smith said.

Russell Conway, a member of the Law Society's Access to Justice committee, evaluated advice provided by CLS Direct in relation to a tenant whose flat (on the Woodberry Down estate in Hackney, east London) was infested by ants. The facts were based on a case of his which settled for £5,000. No legal remedy was suggested by the adviser. Conway described the advice given as 'simply wrong'. The then Department of Constitutional Affairs pointed to impressive customer satisfaction ratings. However, it is possible for a caller to exhibit high levels of satisfaction and still be poorly advised.

CLS – the future

Following Lord Carter's vision of a 'market-driven economy' in legal aid, fixed fees for social welfare law were introduced for civil work in October 2007. It is proving controversial but – at the time of publication – it is too early to take a definitive line other than to agree with the view of the constitutional affairs select committee which described the implementation of fixed fees as a 'breathtaking risk'.[17]

There are many examples where the levels of such fees appear to be too poorly remunerative and the escape provisions too restrictively drawn. For example, the £171 fee for housing work which included homelessness cases. Housing law specialists reckon that the average amount of time for a homelessness case is six hours. This meant under the old system being paid on average £300 for such a case. There is an escape clause at three times that limit but the fear is that most cases will fall between the two.

LAG's view is that standards of casework have fallen since the introduction of fixed fees. Feedback from practitioners supports this view, as does the fact that there have been only a few hundred exceptional case fees claimed (far fewer than expected). The LSC needs to consider reducing the limit at which the exceptional cases regime starts to twice the fixed fee in most cases or consider introducing more graduated fees.

In mental health there is a rate of £791 for all work from initial instructions to taking full instructions, examining medical records and attending at the hearing and subsequently explaining the written decisions and its implications. This comprises £140 for initial instructions (equating to less than two and a half hours under the old hourly rates), £340 for preparation and negotiation, £311 for representation. The Mental Health Lawyers Association makes the point that the same money is to be paid to lawyers representing 'short-term' patients detained only for seven days under s2 of the Mental Health Act 1983 as for cases involving patients sent by the court for detention without limit of time with very lengthy reports and perhaps conflicting psychiatric history.

The LSC insists that three-quarters of firms will be better off. The Mental Health Lawyers Association counters that the new fee regime will 'rapidly accelerate the departure of experienced practitioners from the field to the point where there will be a complete collapse of representation in some, if not large, parts of the country'.

'In the Cold War it was said that the dividing line between the civilised West and the uncivilised East was its treatment of psychiatric patients,' said Richard Charlton. 'The move away from proper legal representation questions where the UK would be in such an equation.' Similar concerns have been expressed in childcare law (see Chapter 6). LAG has no issue with fixed fees provided the level is realistic and the escape provisions are set at a reasonable level.

Meanwhile, the CLS is undergoing a radical shake-up. By 2010, the LSC aims to open CLACs in Barking and Dagenham, Cardiff, East Riding, Gloucestershire, Hull, Manchester, Stockport, Sunderland, Wakefield and West Sussex. They already exist in Gateshead, Leicester, Derby and Portsmouth. At the time of going to press, the LSC has closed the list on CLACs until 2010. The big constraint on their roll-out has proved to be the unwillingness on the part of local authorities to commit to funding legal services.

The CLAC initiative combines the best and worst of recent policy thinking on legal aid. The central idea to have better local planning of services is right but the project appears to be compromised by a crude and divisive tendering process with little respect for the providers.

The role of local authority funding in the CLAC is not defined. It is expected to cover the 'generalist advice service, specialist services for incligible clients and services that are out of scope, notably tribunal representation'. 'However there is no identifiable minimum standard for such services and the specifications for the first five CLACs reveal considerable variation,' wrote Adam Griffith, policy

officer at the Advice Services Alliance. Crispin Passmore, director
of the CLS, has said that the LSC would expect a three-year commitment to funding before going into partnership with a local authority
to form a CLAC. 'But it is for a local authority to decide how much
it wants to fund advice,' he said.[18] 'I wouldn't expect to tell them any
more than I'd expect them to tell us how much we spend on mental
health law or public law.'

The Hull tender illustrated just how controversial and radical the
proposals can be. The contract for the CLAC was won by an out-
of-town bid put together by a private company based in Sheffield,
A4e, in collaboration with the solicitors' firm Howells (also based in
Sheffield). A4e has no track record in legal services other than winning a contract with the CLS to deliver part of its CLS Direct services.
The LSC and Hull City Council will jointly provide £3.5 million for
the Hull CLAC. Hull Citizens Advice (one of the oldest and biggest
bureaux in the network) looks set to lose its two main sources of
funding (£649,000 from the authority and £47,000 from the LSC) in
one go. If an advice agency – a citizens advice bureau, a law centre,
housing or debt service – is not part of the CLAC, then it goes to the
wall or survives in subsistence form. The Hull bureau was set up in
1939 and grew to 57 staff and 75 volunteers by 2008, one of the largest in the Citizens Advice network. It might survive losing the CLAC
contract, but Leicester Law Centre was forced to close in 2008 after its
funding was cut to pay for the new CLAC.

The campaign to save Hull Citizens Advice has attracted much
support – some 10,000 locals signed the bureau's petition. It also
started a debate about the attempt to marry the disparate interests
of funders to provide the elusive CLS 'comprehensive' network. The
two principal funders of local citizens advice bureaux in England and
Wales are local authorities, which in 2007 provided £66 million (46
per cent), and the LSC which provided £30 million (20 per cent).
Clearly, these are very different institutions with differing objectives.
'The LSC's objectives are narrow, whilst those of local authorities em-
brace the concept of community wellbeing. Pooling these two sources
of funding and devising a tender specification which adequately captured both sets of objectives is a major challenge which hasn't been
done successfully,' reflected David Harker, chief executive of Citizens
Advice. 'The result is that insufficient value is placed on the role of
CAB and others in creating viable and cohesive communities.'[19] The
LSC has made it clear that it has little responsibility for those services
that have served the people of Hull for years. A spokeswoman for the
LSC made clear that it 'exists to fund legal aid – rather than other ser-

vices'. 'For too long publicly-funded legal advice has been governed by the structure of the provider base and not by the problems people face. We have taken the decision to design CLACs to meet the needs of clients.' Apparently, whether those clients want them or not.

LAG is not convinced that the CLACs initiative is worth the loss of existing services, however laudable the aim of joining up services. Notwithstanding this, the realpolitik of local authority reluctance to enter into joint tendering means it is unlikely that there will ever be more than a limited number of CLACs.

1   *Observer* 6 August 2006.
2   *Because Britain deserves better*, Labour Party, 1997.
3   Lord Chancellor's Department, *Modernising justice* Cm 4155, TSO, 1998.
4   *Independent* 5 August 2003.
5   *The Community Legal Service: a consultation paper*, May 1999.
6   LSC annual report 2002/03.
7   *Guidance for Community Legal Service Partnerships*, Legal Services Commission, 2000.
8   Department for Constitutional Affairs, *The independent review of the Community Legal Service*, April 2004, para 1.3.1.
9   Advice Services Alliance, 'What are they good for? Advice agencies' experience of Community Legal Service Partnerships', *Independent Lawyer*, May 2004.
10 *Geography of advice*, Citizens Advice, 2004.
11 LAG interview with Richard Collins, June 2008.
12 *Independent Lawyer* October 2006.
13 LSC annual report and accounts 2007/08.
14 Pascoe Pleasence et al, *Causes of action: civil law and social justice*, 2nd edn, TSO, 2006.
15 LSC annual report 2007/08.
16 *Independent Lawyer* July/August 2006.
17 *Implementation of the Carter Review of Legal Aid* HC 223-I, 2007, para 20.
18 *Independent Lawyer* November 2007.
19 *Observer* 28 July 2008.

CHAPTER 6

Family: heading for breakdown

'It is a never-ending carnival of human misery. A ceaseless river of human distress.' That was how Mr Justice Coleridge described the caseload dealt with by the family courts in a speech made in April 2008.[1] 'We are experiencing a period of family meltdown whose effects will be as catastrophic as the meltdown of the ice caps,' he said. The implications posed 'as big a threat to the future of our society as terrorism, street crime or drugs ... What is certain is that almost all of society's social ills can be traced directly to the collapse of the family life.'

The High Court judge, in a speech to family lawyers which was reported widely in the mainstream press, was particularly alarmed at the state of legal aid, which he described as 'withering away'. He accused ministers of being 'determined to pay family lawyers so little they [were] just giving up and turning elsewhere'. The speech reflected widespread dissatisfaction among practitioners.

As discussed in the first two chapters, our system of family legal aid largely grew out of a need for society to meet the demand for advice on divorce. The social upheaval of the two world wars led to a greater demand for accessible legal advice and representation before the courts. Up until the expansion of the legal aid scheme starting in 1973, the main part of the civil caseload comprised family advice relating to divorce. For example, a 1969 survey of legal aid cases in Birmingham found that 86 per cent related to divorce. By 1981 family law still comprised more than two-thirds (67 per cent) of the total of civil work but, due to the overall expansion of legal aid into other areas of civil law, by 1991 it reduced to 43 per cent. The majority of certificated work in civil legal aid (as opposed to generalist legal help) continues to be family work and in 2007 out of a total of 137,963 certificates issued 115,086 were for family law.

Divorcing spouses with little money of their own are often shocked to learn that 'legal aid' is not so much state support as a loan secured on their home which is eventually recovered. Legally-aided clients have to pay a contribution towards the costs or more likely they have a statutory charge put on any money or property 'recovered or preserved in the proceedings'. The latest figures show that £254 million is currently owed to the legal aid fund.[2] In 2005, the government scrapped a rule which allowed the first £3,000 of a person's property to be protected from the charge – effectively making legal aid for divorcing couples a loan for the vast majority of homeowners. Gradually the LSC recovers the money owed to the fund as properties carrying charges for legal aid are sold.

The family law gap

The fall in eligibility levels for legal aid has hit family law badly. Research indicates that around half of the people who could potentially face family law problems are no longer eligible for legal aid.[3] Many of those who are eligible have to make a contribution to legal aid which they can ill afford.

There is growing anecdotal evidence that this is leading to more unrepresented parties in proceedings. In October 2008 Channel 4 News reported on the apparent impact of the introduction of fixed fees on the family courts in child custody. Fixed fees had been introduced 12 months before.[4] Channel 4 obtained a copy of research conducted by the Legal Services Commission (LSC) which found that Northamptonshire County Court reported a seven-fold increase in the number of litigants in person in family cases in that period. It reported that the number of specialist childcare solicitors in the county had more than halved from 15 to seven. If a care order is imposed parents automatically get legal aid, however it might not be available if the order is later challenged or if other relatives are involved.

Anthony Kirk QC, former chairman of the Family Law Bar Association, recalled being rung up by a desperate judge who asked him to work for free because one litigant in person was about to cross-question someone he was accused of abusing. The prospect of, in that case, a grandfather being allowed to cross-examine his grandchildren was 'utterly unthinkable', he said. 'Certainly in a criminal case the Attorney General would have intervened to ensure that that was not going to be allowed to happen and that the grandfather had proper representation.' One family judge (Her Honour Judge Cahill) broke with protocol to offer a view from the Bench reflecting the extent of concern among her fellow judges. 'All a judge can try and do is lend such assistance as they are able to those who are not represented, but of course that has to be dictated by the fact that the judge is there to do justice between the two parties, not to present the case on behalf of one or the other.' When asked if she believed everyone has a right to representation, Judge Cahill said: 'Certainly'.

Channel 4 noted that ministers were consulting to reduce the budget for family barristers by an extra £13 million. This was a reference to the LSC and Ministry of Justice review of the graduated fee scheme and, in particular, whether to scrap the difference in rates between advocates and solicitors.

It is an example of how effective an advocate the Bar can be in its own cause. LAG has taken issue with the Bar on this point. It argues that the scheme is one area of publicly funded family advice that could possibly be cut without prejudicing the quality of legal representation in court. The family graduated fee scheme was introduced in May 2001 based on fixed rates for specific activities depending on the complexity and length of a case. The LSC pointed out that one quarter of the £2 billion legal aid budget was spent on family cases and about 18 per cent was paid to barristers through the graduated fee scheme. Total expenditure on the scheme was £74.2 million in 2003/04 and rose to £98.2 million in 2007/08.

Even the Family Law Bar Association has accepted the principle of 'equal pay for equal work', but argued that the LSC proposals failed to 'appreciate the distinction between simple and complex hearings'. A standoff with the solicitors' profession ensued. The Law Society accused the Bar of 'shameless self interest' in trying to preserve the pay differential, arguing that the 'suggestion that solicitors only perform simple advocacy whilst barristers only perform more complex work' was 'untenable'.

It was an issue that LAG explored. The LSC provided LAG with fully-costed examples illustrating the rationale behind the different ways in which the two sides of the profession are remunerated. In an interim hearing in a public law case, the barrister was paid £446 and the solicitor £228. In the second example, a final hearing in a private law child case, the costs were £692 and £508 respectively. The calculations came from the LSC with heavy caveats and were 'illustrative rather than absolute'. 'Perhaps the most sensible observation from this exercise is the arbitrary way that these figures appear to be arrived at,' noted LAG. 'It is neither sensible nor transparent and, frankly, neither is the discrepancy in pay between Bar and solicitors.'

Family law practitioners claim to have been particularly badly hit by the fixed fees introduced in October 2007. 'Many child care law experts predict financial ruin for child care lawyers and, more worrying, disaster for the children they represent,' wrote David Emmerson, a past chair of the Legal Aid Practitioners Group and chair of Resolution's legal aid committee.[5] The number of firms undertaking family legal aid has declined to 2,735 in 2008 from 4,593 in 2001 (with almost one-third undertaking less than 1 per cent of the work).

There has been concern from practitioners about clients having access to legal aid lawyers. The Association of Lawyers for Children claimed that one-third of practitioners and 40 per cent of law firms planned to reduce their reliance on legal aid as a response to the introduction of fixed fees. Family law practitioners (unlike most other types of legal aid lawyer) are well-placed to vote with their feet and switch from legal aid rates to more generous private rates.

The practitioner experience is strikingly at odds with the oft-repeated assertion along the lines that '97% of the eligible population have access to a family legal-aid provider within 45 minutes' travel time on public transport'.[6] The meaningfulness of such a claim is something that LAG would challenge. Proximity is no measure of willingness of such firms to take on the work nor capacity to take such work on. If someone is being beaten up by his or her partner the fact that there is a solicitor within 45 minutes is no help if the solicitor cannot (or will not) take the case on.

Childcare experts have also been alarmed about the implication of government policy to make courts self-financing. Local authority social services departments from 2008 were asked to meet the full cost of care proceedings through court fees of £4,000 (previously they were £150) and £4,825 if a case goes to a full hearing. The idea is to recover the £35 million costs and plough them back into the court system.

The Court Service consultation, which featured the controversial plans, argued that social services were 'subject to a clear statutory duty to protect the interests of children'.[7] 'It would be unlawful for them to avoid taking court proceedings for financial reasons,' it said. 'Nor, given that the local authority spending settlement reflects the additional pressure, is there any reason to think they would do so.' The government announced it would increase funding by £40 million 'so there should be no impact on vulnerable children'. Local authorities have acknowledged that neither is the money likely to be adequate nor would it be specifically assigned to care cases.

The judiciary has been outspoken. District Judge Nick Crichton denounced the plans as 'illogical, if not absurd' and 'a massive disincentive' for cases involving children suffering persistent neglect to come before the courts. 'The concept that a local authority should pay for access to the courts, for access to justice on behalf of children, is illogical if not absurd,' commented Judge Crichton, who sits at the Inner London Family Proceedings Court.

> The state has a responsibility to protect the public from criminals. Nobody would suggest that the police and CPS should pay a fee to do that because they're an arm of the state meeting the state's responsibility. In family proceedings, the state has a responsibility to protect vulnerable children. Why should the local authority have to pay a fee to have access to the court any more than the police or prosecuting authorities?[8]

It is a compelling argument and one that LAG supports.

Applications for child care and supervision orders have dropped by 25 per cent since the rule change. Just 1,611 applications were made by councils in England and Wales between the beginning of April 2008 and the end of July compared with 2,160 in the same period in 2007 and 2,284 between April and July 2006.[9]

The drop-off is not solely explained by the fee increase but also because of new measures requiring councils to do more preparatory work known as the Public Law Outline (PLO), introduced in April 2008. The PLO replaced the protocol for judicial management in public law Children Act cases and was designed to reduce unnecessary delay and promote better co-operation between the parties involved in care and supervision orders. This has led to the front-loading of cases and more active judicial management. It is hoped that this new policy will lead to fewer cases going to court and, provided there are the resources to deal with cases properly, this should result in fewer care proceedings being issued.

To make a decision in such cases, expert reports and adequate professional scrutiny is needed. A pre-action meeting under the new PLO procedure will usually need to consider parenting, psychological and psychiatric assessment reports. Reports cost on average between £2,000 and £3,000 (costs which are again to be met by cash-strapped local authorities). In this procedure parents can be represented by a solicitor on a fixed fee (£347, in 2008) – which practitioners argue is insufficient for the work involved.[10]

There is also a yawning gap in services for women who are victims of domestic violence. Many do not apply for injunctions to protect themselves from violent partners due to a lack of awareness about their rights or through fear of taking such action. New Labour heralded its Domestic Violence, Crime and Victims Act 2004 as the 'biggest overhaul of legislation on domestic violence in 30 years'. The legislation gave the police powers to make common assault, where the victim only fears violence, an arrestable offence. The courts were also given the power to jail defendants for five years for breaching a non-molestation order. However, a 2008 evaluation of its success concluded that its impact was 'limited'. The study looked at the experience in Croydon and South Tyneside and found that convictions for domestic violence had fallen to a three-year low. According to the study: 'Those engaged with the court process felt there had been a reduction in applications for non-molestation orders and orders granted since July 2007 either due to both a reduction in the availability of legal aid and the criminalisation of breaches, or because victims were concerned about potential imprisonment that follows a breach.'

According to the LSC's own research undertaken in 2005, 45,000 women who were victims of domestic violence and a further 250,000 with relationship problems took no action.[11] There is strong evidence that there are not solicitor services available even for the women who wish to take legal action. Citizens Advice highlighted the gaps in provision in 2008.[12] By way of an illustration, they featured the case of a woman who had been the victim of domestic abuse and who approached her local bureau in the West Midlands. Although the LSC listed ten solicitors in her area that would apparently take such cases on, none were available when they were approached. Instead, the only solicitor able to take the case insisted on undertaking it on a fee-paying basis. Two police stations in the local area also complained that they could not find solicitors willing to take domestic violence cases funded by legal aid. A vivid illustration of the point made before in this chapter that proximity to a legal aid lawyer is no measure of 'access to justice'.

The Commission for Equality and Human Rights has also highlighted the general lack of availability of support services for women who are victims of domestic violence.[13] The LSC has conceded that there might be gaps in provision and promised to look at more innovative ways of filling these, for example by expanding telephone advice, supported where necessary by representation services.

A survey of black, minority ethnic and refugee women with civil legal problems conducted by Rights of Women found that over one-third (35 per cent) had problems relating to domestic violence and a similar share (37 per cent) related to contact and residence orders.

The survey, conducted in 2007, of 327 women who rang the organisation's advice line found that 70 per cent were unsatisfied or very unsatisfied with the legal aid system. This figure, which included those women who failed to qualify for legal aid, indicates considerable frustration with legal aid and nearly one-third indicated that there was poor availability of local legal services.

The Rights of Women service is itself evidence of unmet demand. In 2007 it received 90,000 calls but was only able to advise 1,710 people. There is an acute problem in relation to domestic violence work. Some practitioners tell LAG in private that it makes poor business sense to take on such cases. By its nature, injunction work involves dropping ongoing work in order to issue the proceedings. Practitioners are less likely to do this, arguing they do not have the free capacity to take on the work due to their commitments to existing clients.

Joined up thinking?

New Labour launched its Family Advice and Information Networks (FAINs) in 2001 aimed at promoting mediation in family law disputes and integrating legal and specialist support services. Clients would discuss an action plan at the first meeting with their solicitor, drawing together the different aspects of their case including mediation, counselling and other legal services such as debt advice. The idea was that clients could take this statement away with them (the LSC had a pro forma) and it would assist in their movement between agencies.

It quickly became apparent in a six-month 'pre-pilot' period in 2002 which took place in five areas that it would not be possible to establish networks without extra resources as solicitors had difficulties building working relationships with outside agencies.

By 2004, the LSC watered down the proposal, renaming it the Family Advice and Information Service – FAInS (as opposed to FAINs). The LSC was careful to explain that this slightest of name changes did 'not imply any lessening of its commitment to developing networks of support', instead saying that the change of emphasis '[took] the onus away from family solicitors as the only professionals responsible for developing them'.

The Newcastle University Centre for Family Studies evaluated the pilot, comparing data from more than 1,000 cases pre-FAInS and a similar number in the FAInS period. It concluded that there were no discernible differences in information received by clients or referrals to other agencies such as those offering support related to victims of domestic violence. In fact, there were fewer referrals for mediation after the introduction of FAInS and so that particular innovation had no impact in promoting better communication between the parties.

The study did make a number of positive findings. It concluded that solicitors involved in FAInS did promote resolving disputes by conciliation and settlement rather than going to court. A useful contribution given the consistent feedback LAG has received from family law practitioners who view court proceedings as a last resort for clients. The main flaw in the referral system was that the service was limited to informing the clients of their options for other services but without a meaningful link to those services to secure appointments for clients to follow through with the advice. To that extent, the research adds to the evidence base supporting the community legal advice centres initiative in tackling clients' 'clusters' of problems.[14]

Access to justice in family and childcare cases is a part of the legal aid machinery where there appear to be particular problems. It is not meeting the needs of clients. The PLO and the hike in fees have had an impact on the number of cases entering the system. Urgent research needs to be commissioned to explore the serious concerns raised that children are not receiving the same level of protection as under the previous system. Separately there are severe pressures faced by family law practitioners and evidence suggests that many are leaving publicly funded law for more remunerative private client work. It is clear that there are gaps and these are likely to be exacerbated as fewer cases and the squeeze on profits caused by fixed fees forces more firms out of legal aid work.

1   Resolution National Conference, 5 April 2008.

2   LSC annual report and accounts 2007/08 p53.

3   Pascoe Pleasence, Nigel Balmer and Tania Tam, *Civil justice in England and Wales. Report of the 2006 English and Welsh civil and social justice survey*, LSC, 2007.

4   Channel 4 News, 21 October 2008.

5   *Solicitor Journal* 13 May 2008, p7.

6   David Godfrey, Executive Director, Corporate Services, LSC, letter to the *Guardian*, 28 May 2008.

7   *The Community Legal Service: a consultation paper*, May 1999.

8   *Independent Lawyer* February 2008.

9   According to figures from the Children and Family Court Advisory Support Service (Cafcass) as reported in *Law Society Gazette* 21 August 2008.

10 LAG predicts that sometime in 2009 the numbers of cases are likely to reach 80–90% of the numbers in the period before the introduction of the PLO (which would indicate that the PLO has had a positive impact on reducing the numbers of cases going to court).

11 Pascoe Pleasence et al, *Causes of action: civil law and social justice*, 2nd edn, TSO, 2006.

12 Virendra Sharma MP, 'Government support for domestic violence organisations', 8 May 2008.

13 Equality and Human Rights Commission and End Violence Against Women Campaign, *Map of gaps: the postcode lottery of violence against women support services*, 2007.

14 See Chapter 5.

CHAPTER 7

Personal injury: accident waiting to happen

Twins Ben and Sam Boreham from Ruislip, Middlesex set off for Old Trafford, home of Manchester United, with their family just a couple of days before their eighth birthday in 1998. They were travelling with big brother Dean, mother Jane, and her best friend Debbie.

What should have been one of the most exciting trips of their lives – a birthday treat for two David Beckham-obsessed boys – ended in tragedy when their car smashed into an unlit vehicle abandoned in the middle lane of the M1 outside Watford Gap. The driver of the other car was sitting stunned on the grass verge having crashed into the central reservation moments earlier having fallen asleep at the wheel.

The family was lucky to survive. Sam suffered brain injuries and his left femur was shattered, Ben was effectively scalped, Dean broke his collarbone and they were all deeply traumatised.

The Boreham case has been cited as a tragic example of the new era of 'no win, no fee'. Talking in 2005 to the *Observer*, Jane Boreham said that there had been many times since that night when she has wished that she had not survived.[1] 'This time last year I nearly drove my car into a brick wall because I got to the point where I just couldn't go on anymore,' she said. Jane described Sam as 'a 14-year-old body with a nine-year old brain'. 'He doesn't really have the common sense to do what his peers do and so he struggles at school, doesn't make friends easily and he's seeing a psychologist for post-traumatic stress. It's a lot to deal with.'

Sam's problems had a knock-on effect on his twin. 'Ben doesn't really cope and resents Sam for holding him back,' she said. 'They argue from the moment they wake up to the moment they go to bed.' The consequences of that night in 1998 would have been bad enough but their tragedy was compounded because the compensation that should have lightened their load was siphoned off. The compensation claims of Ben, Dean and their mother were eventually settled and Sam has received a series of interim payments; but a non-qualified claims assessor, Steve Edwards (not his real name), had first taken a cut of 20 per cent plus VAT. The family bitterly regrets the deal they signed up to in a hospital waiting room after their son woke from a four-day coma.

In 2000, New Labour embarked upon a huge gamble. In one fell swoop, ministers scrapped legal aid for routine personal injury cases, appealing to entrepreneurial law firms and a new breed of non-lawyer claims companies to fill the newly-created access to justice gap. Such firms would run accident victims' claims on a new type of 'no win, no fee' deal.

This heralded a number of developments in our legal landscape attracting huge controversy. The move intensified concerns about the so-called 'compensation culture' in the UK (or, at the least, the perception of it). That in itself suggests increased access to justice albeit at the expense of the quality of legal advice. Other developments were far more capable of proof. Genuine accident victims lost out as damages were consumed by the exorbitant fees and charges associated with the new complex arrangements. Meanwhile many unmeritorious claims were being generated by new style claims companies and lawyers spotting a new potential to make money.

Alison Eddy, a solicitor at the claimant firm Irwin Mitchell, took over the Boreham case after the distraught mother was referred to them by a barrister-friend from a church group. Eddy was appalled by the claim farmer's conduct and the way in which he 'exploited a vulnerable family'. In 2005 when the *Observer* caught up with Steve Edwards, he was extremely reluctant to let a lucrative client slip. Edwards was ringing up Jane Boreham nine times a day and even threatened to make the family homeless. He told Eddy that he wanted his 20 per cent cut regardless who was advising the client. The solicitor warned him that she would bring a claim under prevention of harassment legislation unless he left the Borehams alone. 'The last time we spoke was the Monday before Christmas and he was saying that he was going to put a charge on the house to protect his cut of any future compensation,' a distraught Jane recalled in 2005.

The Boreham family last heard from Edwards in September 2007. The final payout for Sam is likely to exceed £1 million (his claim cannot be resolved until his education has been concluded). 'The claim is a complex one and the presence of this unregulated claims assessor has added to the stress of a family who have had to endure enough,' Alison Eddy says. 'For him, one family's tragic misfortune is a means to make money. He was allowed to operate in an unregulated vacuum – accident victims deserve better. They need protection.'

Plugging the personal injury gap

Within four years of scrapping legal aid, 130,000 people contacted citizens advice bureaux with problems they claimed to have suffered as a result of rogue claims companies in the period after legal aid was withdrawn from personal injury. The changes ushered in what has been described as a new age of 'legal market capitalism'.

Successive governments since the 1980s had been toying with a conundrum: how to withdraw legal aid without removing access to justice for the ordinary person? That debate should be seen in the context of increasing numbers of people disqualified from legal aid. According to a report by the London School of Economics, nine million adults fell out of scope for personal injury between 1972 and 1989.[2]

The legal profession and government had previously both been extremely wary of 'no win, no fee' despite debate through the 1970s and 1980s about the viability of the kind of contingency fees which had been in operation in the US since 1850. Under these arrangements the losing party would be required to pay the successful opponent's costs (in other words, the 'loser pays' rule did not apply). The lawyer takes a percentage cut of the damages.

The 1979 Royal Commission on Legal Services (the Benson commission) concluded that a change in the law to give lawyers a direct financial interest in the outcome of the case was not in the public interest. Ministers accepted the recommendation in 1983 but five years later both the Civil Justice Review and the Marre report recommended that the issue should be looked at again. In 1989 the government published a consultative green paper to examine whether the restrictions on the use of contingency fees should be lifted.[3] The overwhelming response was negative. A white paper published later that year rejected contingency fees but introduced the concept of conditional fees.[4] Contingency fees, it was argued, would 'create an unacceptable degree of conflict of interest between the lawyer and his client which could result in his being unable to give the client or the court advice of the required degree of impartiality'. There was little objection to funding based on the Scottish method of 'speculative' actions though. If the case was lost, the lawyers were paid nothing and if they won they would receive the usual fee. Lawyers had been conducting litigation on this basis since the 18th century.

Conditional fees were introduced under Courts and Legal Services Act 1990 in 1995. Such agreements allowed a lawyer to take on a case on the understanding that if the case was lost the lawyer would not charge for the work done; if however the case was won, the lawyer was entitled to charge a success fee calculated as a percentage of normal costs to recompense him or her for the 'risk' of not being paid. Thus the conditional fee agreement (CFA) allowed lawyers and clients to share the risks of litigation.

The idea was that the 'success fee' should reflect the degree of risk the lawyer was taking – the higher the chance of winning, the lower the success fee and vice versa. The 1990 Act allowed the Lord Chancellor to make orders specifying the proceedings in which such agreements could be made and excluded areas, such as criminal and family proceedings. The Lord Chancellor of the time, Lord Mackay of Clashfern, allowed conditional fees for personal injury, insolvency and cases before the European Commission and the European Court of Human Rights. He also prescribed the type of information that a CFA needed to contain. The Law Society produced its own guidance for solicitors using conditional fees as well as a model agreement. It advised solicitors to apply a voluntary limit on the proportion of damages that could be taken by the success fee and suggested this should be no more than 25 per cent. It also arranged a scheme of insurance for clients to cover meeting the opponents' costs fixed at affordable premiums (starting at £92 and going up to £155).

The judiciary and Bar remained hostile. As Lord Mackay was drawing up his plans for 'no win, no fee' in 1995, the barrister-writer John Mortimer QC complained bitterly about the lack of independence conditional fees would bring. His famous creation Horace Rumpole had memorably, and fondly, described himself as 'an elderly black taxi cab, standing waiting on the rank, ready to pick up any customer who's prepared to pay what's on the clock, or have it paid for him by legal aid'.[5] Mortimer (while acknowledging that the analogy suggested another, even older profession prepared to 'service the most unlovable and indeed the most repellent clientele') cited this as the reason why his professional colleagues could not stomach 'no win, no fee'.

'We should, suggests Lord Mackay, encourage lawyers to gamble on the results of litigation. If they are successful they can double their fees, he explained, and if they are unsuccessful they charge the client nothing,' the author continued. 'Across the Atlantic, lawyers back civil cases in the way that theatrical impresarios put on musicals.'

The ambivalence of the Bar towards 'no win, no fee' is reflected in the Bar Council's guidance on conditional fees. It considers situations in which some barristers and chambers might find it appropriate to enter into agreements with each other to work under CFAs as a set or in groups in order to 'spread the risk'. 'However, there are some barristers and sets of chambers who will not consider it appropriate to work under CFA at all or who will only consider it appropriate to work under them on a one-off basis for each particular CFA ... It is important to ensure that no arrangement or agreement is entered into which compromises or appears to compromise a barrister's integrity or independence ... or which creates or appears to create a conflict of interest.'[6] The personal injury Bar has had little choice but to accept CFAs or else stop practising. That said, it appears to have embraced 'no win, no fee' with considerable enthusiasm and it has proved to be a lucrative practice area. As one commentator has put it, though, there persists a general feeling at the Bar that CFAs are 'all a bit grubby and we would rather it had never happened'.

In one fell swoop

Solicitors took to the new funding scheme with some enthusiasm. In 1997, when conditional fees had been available for 30 months, around 34,000 supporting insurance policies had been issued. However, there was some caution. The Policy Studies Institute was commissioned to review the new scheme and raised serious questions about solicitors' abilities to assess risk. It noted: 'The uplift appears to be either too low or (more often) too high, in almost half the cases, than would be justified to compensate the solicitor for losing the case.' That same research found that in 99 per cent of cases insurance was taken out and in almost all cases the Law Society's Accident Line Protect scheme was used. At the time, LAG predicted that there was unlikely to be a great rush of lawyers willing to work on CFAs outside personal injury. 'CFAs are largely ineffective without appropriately priced insurance products to protect against liability costs,' it noted. The Chancery Lane-endorsed scheme was affordable because it was restricted to firms with proven experience in handling personal injury cases and because it was relatively easy to measure risk in such areas of work. Accident Line Protect's brokers themselves acknowledged that it would be 'extremely difficult' to produce a viable scheme to cover general litigation.

New Labour's enthusiasm for CFAs to take a huge load of work out of the legally-aided scheme gathered pace under Lord Irvine's Lord Chancellorship – notwithstanding his description when in opposition of 'no win no fee' as 'another gimmick to avoid state responsibility and secure justice on the cheap'. The received wisdom in the profession at least was that removing personal injury from legal aid would not deliver such a huge saving, not least when compared to the apparent risk to which it exposed accident victims. Robert Marshall Andrews QC, the Labour MP and lawyer, argued that publicly funded personal injury was 'the most efficient of all public services'. 'Of £220 million spent per annum, 80% is recovered from costs of unsuccessful defendants, a figure which in itself pays tribute to the integrity and quality of the advice,' he said. 'The net cost is even less as the damages remove victims from welfare and their families from the famous dependency culture.' The then Lord Chancellor, Lord Irvine, while acknowledging that legal aid was 'a highly successful public social service', noted that, in the case of personal injury, it was 'conspicuously successful'.

In 1999/2000, in personal injury's last year in the legal aid scheme, the Legal Services Commission (LSC) paid out £178.3 million and recouped £124.7 million leaving a net cost of £53.5 million – the following year there was a net cost of £35.1 million, and £10.7 million the year after, then a net gain in 2002/03 of £10.3 million. The cash influx allowed the LSC to make eligibility increases.

In Lord Irvine's speech to the Law Society's annual conference in Cardiff in October 1997 he was determined to – as he put it – 'face down the vested interests'.[7] 'Legal aid has become a leviathan with a ferocious appetite,' he began. The Lord Chancellor proposed to extend conditional fees to most civil cases for money or damages. He posed the question: should legal aid also be offered in cases where other arrangements (in other words, conditional fees) already existed to support litigants? 'I think not,' he replied, somewhat pre-empting the consultation he had just announced. Irvine also flagged up the idea of a Contingent Legal Aid Fund (CLAF), to plug the gaps for the less well off who could not obtain advice under the new 'no win, no fee' regime. The idea behind a CLAF is that cases are supported and funded on the basis that a percentage of the damages recovered is paid back to a self-financing fund. Lord Irvine declared that he had 'major concerns' on the grounds that only the weak cases will be supported by a CLAF 'because lawyers would prefer to cream off the stronger cases'.

The Lord Chancellor was on bullish form when it came to the

introduction of 'no win, no fee' and not afraid of upsetting those vested interests. The language in an article he penned for the *New Statesman* was telling.[8] It suggested removing public funding from personal injury was straightforward. 'Making justice affordable', wrote Lord Irvine, 'simply involves the determination to modernise, by extending "no-win, no-fee" arrangements to all civil proceedings except family cases. At a stroke, legal help would become affordable in disputes with banks, builders and insurance companies, provided the lawyer had sufficient confidence in the case to enter a "no win, no fee" agreement.'

The 'as yet untested' willingness of insurers to step in was brusquely dealt with. 'Insurers are already showing interest in covering the risk of having to pay the other sides' costs,' he said. At that point Accident Line Protect was the only product on the market. The Lord Chancellor went on to describe the 'second challenge of modernising legal aid' as being 'not so easy' – that was overcoming the 'heavy impediment' that was the 'entrenched interests of the legal professions'. 'Not surprisingly, they are attached to the old regime because it is designed to cater for the idiosyncratic ways they do business and to deliver a healthy income from the taxpayer,' he said.

Enter the claims company

On 1 April 2000, legal aid for personal injury cases was abolished. The fate of accident victims was in the hands of market forces. New payment rules for solicitors working on a 'no win, no fee' basis were introduced as part of the Access to Justice Act 1999. Lord Irvine aimed to solve the perceived deficiencies of the original model of CFA by allowing for recovery of the insurance premium plus success fee from the losing party rather than having those two costs swallowing up the damages.

There quickly sprung to life a generation of claims companies. Non-lawyer claims management companies already dealt with mainly straightforward accident cases – such as road traffic accidents, slip and trip claims, and injuries at work. They ranged from those that dealt with all aspects of a case through to simple referral schemes that put clients in touch with law firms. The model that quickly became prevalent in the wake of the Access to Justice Act used marketing might to drum up claims through TV advertising campaigns and then, if necessary, passed them on to law firms which they arranged on panels. It was the old Claims Direct (not to be confused with the new 'Claims Direct' as the name is now used by the claimant firm Russell Jones & Walker for its claims management operation) that led the way and quickly became a household name as a result of a saturation TV advertising campaign inspired by aggressive US marketing tactics. The old Claims Direct and then The Accident Group briefly blazed the trail for the claims farmers.

Claims Direct was the first company to exploit a lucrative business opportunity from new style 'no win, no fee' deals but it soon spawned legions of copycat companies. Its name quickly embedded itself into the public consciousness because of its daytime TV advertising campaign. The company deployed legions of young reps with clipboards in shopping centres and cold-called at people's homes. Claims Direct represented a tidal wave of litigation – at its peak signing up 5,000 new clients a month.

It quickly became apparent that many accident victims were being ill-served by this new breed of claims company. They were finding to their cost that 'no win, no fee' was a deceptively simple expression – it did not mean 'win, no cost'. Many legitimate accident victims with successful claims had their damages swallowed by the exorbitant costs of claims companies and their lawyers.

However, the City was impressed with the potential for this newly privatised part of the legal system. Claims Direct floated in July 2000 and its founders, ex-cabbie Tony Sullman and solicitor Colin Poole, were reported to have pocketed £50 million and £10 million respectively. Two years later the company went bust. The Accident Group followed shortly after.

The unexpurgated story of the demise of Claims Direct was revealed in a September 2002 ruling by the senior costs judge Peter Hurst in what became known as the 'Claims Direct' test cases. He held that only half of its £1,250 insurance premium was recoverable from defendant insurers. The ruling exposed a flawed business model that might have seduced the City but was to be their undoing.

Claims Direct's first scheme ran between 1996 and 1999 and was predicated on the simple principle that the company would take 30 per cent of any damages recovered and pay for the opponent's costs if the claim were to fail. Sullman and Poole began looking into flotation in March 1999, however, according to senior costs judge Hurst, they were advised by their accountants that flotation would be 'handicapped' by 'the contingent liabilities' of the 30 per cent scheme. So they scrapped it and brought in insurers. The relaunched product had a £1,250 'insurance premium' that included insurance costs of only £140. Share prices leapt from 180p to 353p in its first two months.

The only problem was that the defendant insurance industry refused to foot the bill. The so called 'costs war' between the defendant insurers and the claimant side was to become a feature of the post-'Access to Justice' world.

According to the judgment, no sooner had Claims Direct floated than it was 'rocking from one disaster to another'. The extent to which the company and its City backers got their sums wrong is revealed in the judgment. The underwriters had worked on the assumption of a failure rate of cases of between 4 and 6 per cent (optimists at Claims Direct put it at 3 per cent or less), but in reality it was 25 per cent.

The Accident Group had a similarly dramatic demise. The company's boss Mark Langford became a byword for corporate insensitivity when he sacked his 2,700 workforce by text ('unfortunately salaries not paid – please do not contact office – full details to follow later today').

The Accident Group illustrates the accident claim 'gold rush'. It was reckoned that it conquered 25 per cent of the personal injury market in less than two years. The company claimed to be one of the fastest-growing UK businesses and reported an increase in turnover of 179 per cent in 2002 to £243 million. In June 2003, its parent company, the Amulet Group, announced that it was to go into administration following 'continual battles with the insurance industry'. The courts similarly trashed the Accident Group business model. Senior costs judge Hurst halved the premium from £997.50 to £450 and also ruled that a fee of £310 paid by the Accident Group's panel firms to the company could not be recovered. At the time of going to press, the fall-out still reverberates with the insurer AXA pursuing legal action against 78 law firms to recoup £60 million losses associated with after-the-event policies and a further 100 law firms could be drawn in.[9] Action against 600 TAG panel firms concluded in 2008.

No win, no fee, no chance ...

What have been the consumers' experiences of claims companies? In fact, there has been little research into such a controversial way of funding cases. 'Misunderstandings about CFAs were widespread,' concluded a report by Stella Yarrow and Pamela Abrams in 1999.[10] 'They concern not only the finer points but the fundamental building blocks of the scheme.' That report demonstrated the complexity of the pre-Access to Justice Act version of CFAs but noted that clients generally 'misunderstood the central premise of CFAs – that the solicitors risk not being paid at all and that the success fee compensates them for this risk'. The study interviewed 40 clients and only one (who had 'considerable previous experience of the legal system') understood how conditional fees worked in their entirety. It also reported that some lawyers did not know how they worked.

Citizens advice bureaux had to bear the brunt of the Claims Direct/ Accident Group onslaught. In a 2004 report, Citizens Advice concluded that personal injury compensation was 'failing consumers', making a similar point to the 1999 research. 'The complex financial and legal processes involved are often misunderstood by consumers and consumers' needs can be misunderstood by the service providers,' it said, adding that there was 'widespread mis-selling of legal and insurance products, and consumers are often induced into signing conditional fee agreements inappropriately'.[11]

The problem centred on the complexity of 'no win, no fee'. According to Citizens Advice consumers were often 'misled into thinking the system would be genuinely "no win, no fee"' but could often 'find that costs are hidden and unpredictable' and that 'loan-financed insurance premiums, in addition to other legal costs' eroded any pay-outs. 'In some cases consumers even owe money at the end of the process,' it noted. The report cited one example concerning a man from Lancashire who had an accident at work and was awarded £1,250. Despite winning his case, the interest on the loan he took out to pay for insurance, plus his solicitor's bill, meant that he was left with a debt of nearly £2,400. The actions of claims companies fell outside any regulatory regime yet, Citizens Advice noted, 'they are increasingly the primary introducer of the consumer to the claims process as well as a complex package of financial services – consequently the information and advice they give is of critical significance to the consumer'.

There was no need for accident victims to lose a penny. At the time of the Citizens Advice report one law firm network (Injury Lawyers4U) promised 'there'll be no deductions when you receive your settlement cheque, just 100% compensation' – a pledge made by many individual firms as well.

Citizens Advice also noted that consumers were being subjected to 'high-pressure' sales tactics by 'unqualified intermediaries' and practices included approaching accident victims in hospitals. Concerns about the antics of some claims companies had long alarmed consumer groups. In November 2002 BBC's 'Watchdog' installed a secret camera to catch an Accident Group rep exhorting a prospective client to put in a bogus claim for a bus crash when he was actually at home ('Lee Loughman ... an ordinary man living in an ordinary street ... with some extraordinary powers. He can fall off kerbs while watching television; he can even be in bus crashes without leaving the house').

The industry body, the Claims Standard Council, reported in 2006 on how children in hospitals or GPs' surgeries were whiling away anxious moments with 'brain-teasers' planted by one company (the Nationwide Accident Services).[12] The word-search puzzle invited youngsters to ring words in a box of jumbled up letters, including 'compensation', 'claim today' and 'no win, no fee'. It also reported that two of the company's reps, hanging around hospital waiting rooms 'pretending to be doctors wearing white coats and [carrying] a clipboard', were approaching patients and offering them £200 for a claim.

The 2004 Citizens Advice report also criticised lawyers. It noted 'cherry-picking of high value cases with high chances of success'. 'This results in lawyers refusing to take on good small claims which may nevertheless be of enormous financial and personal significance to the client, thus denying access to justice,' it noted. 'Although the former system of funding personal injury claims only represented a net cost to the public of 4 per cent of legal aid annual expenditure, we do not advocate a simple return to public funding for personal injury cases based on current legal aid eligibility criteria.' Legal aid was 'very restricted and means tested', it noted, and 'by definition was not actually of assistance to many consumers'.

Many of the worst excesses of the first few years following the Access to Justice Act were eventually curbed as a result of the demise of the two market leaders, regulation through the courts, and perhaps a degree of industry self-regulation through the Claims Standard Council. Even so it had quickly become apparent that there was a compelling case for a proper, statutory regulatory scheme, but the government – perhaps, fearful of driving new entrants out of the market – stalled despite the clamour.

Claims management regulation came into force in April 2007 when it became an offence to provide such services without authorisation. The trading standards department of Staffordshire County Council was assigned to police a notoriously unruly sector. Mark Boleat, formerly director general of the Association of British Insurers, became head of claims management regulation at the Department for Constitutional Affairs. The watchdog was not just looking at personal injury, but dealing with concerns about claims companies profiting from mis-selling scandals (most notably endowment policies in the 1980s and 1990s).

It is widely seen to be a light touch regulatory regime albeit maybe one commensurate with the proportions of the problem. Although according to its 2008 annual report, 1,385 businesses are author-ised with the claims management regulator with a total turnover of £173,934,677. At the time of going to press, some 74 companies had their authorisation suspended. The watchdog has reported that cold calling has been 'significantly reduced', marketing in hospitals and misleading use of the expression 'no win, no fee' have both 'largely been eliminated'.

The controversial funding mechanism clearly provides access to justice to many people. Many claimant lawyers including the Asso-ciation of Personal Injury Lawyers argue, perhaps unsurprisingly, that it works without a hitch in the great majority of cases. '"No win, no fee" arrangements are vital in helping to give the public a voice in courts', said the justice minister Bridget Prentice launching 2008 research into conditional fees.[13] 'However, we are aware of growing concerns that they may not always be operating in the interests of access to justice.'

Such research is urgently needed to establish what kind of service consumers are receiving. Citizens Advice in 2008 believes that many of the concerns raised in their 2004 research persist despite the ex-tinction of the two discredited market leaders. The group sticks to its initial advice of scrapping conditional fees and introducing contin-gency fees.

Certainly, there is need for scrutiny, but LAG is as yet uncon-vinced of the case to abolish conditional fees. Further research is needed otherwise the reform agenda is in danger of being deter-mined by anecdotal evidence. One consequence of the rise of the claims company has been huge increases in the payment of referral fees. It is reckoned that solicitors pay around £500 to £700 to buy a personal injury claim (ironically much higher than in the days of Claims Direct or The Accident Group). The consumer is not aware of this payment which is made not only to claims companies but also to liability insurers. It makes 'no win, no fee' even more opaque and raises questions about the independence of legal advice – how hard will a lawyer fight for a case that he or she has already spent a few hundred pounds acquiring?

Insurance companies are reported to be increasingly setting up 'third party capture' units through which they try to settle the claims of injured people before they take independent legal advice. In 2008, the Association of Personal Injury Lawyers sent evidence to MPs including a claim on behalf of bereaved parents who lost their three children in a road traffic accident. They were originally offered £21,000 by one insurer over a claim that was settled for £60,000. The insurance industry acknowledges that 'third-party capture' is increasingly part of its business model as, insurers argue, a direct response to the increasing cost of processing claims. They argue that going directly to accident victims is a way of simply cutting out an expensive middle-man – the lawyer.

'No win, no fee' might be an innovation that the legal profession has learned to live with (with varying degrees of enthusiasm) and around which a new claims industry has been created, but LAG has concerns about how well it serves consumers.

Outside mainstream personal injury, there is considerable doubt about access to justice, especially in complex group actions and litigation where after-the-event insurance is either unavailable or not affordable.

In 2008 for the first time CFA-funded clinical negligence claims have exceeded publicly funded ones. The reasons for this are various. Claimant lawyers complain of the bureaucracy of legal aid and having to subject themselves to the perceived 'micromanagement' of cases by the LSC. Often clients are asked by the LSC to make a contribution and running a case on a CFA avoids that. However, there is of course the potential to make money on a good case – and so why wouldn't a claimant lawyer opt for 'no win, no fee'?

The conditional fee after-the-event market has 'definitely matured', according to Action for the Victims of Medical Accident. The difficult areas are low value claims and cases where there are fatalities, reports the group's legal director Fiona Freedland.

The public funding of class actions in complex product liability cases has long been identified as a problem area. The fate of the UK Vioxx litigants is seen by many as representative of the uphill battles that group litigants face. In November 2007 the manufacturer Merck announced plans to pay more than $4.85 billion to alleged American victims of the anti-arthritis drug who claim to have suffered heart attacks and strokes as a result of it. It is reckoned to be the biggest settlement of its kind.

UK claimants took their legal action to Merck's backyard in New Jersey, bypassing the UK court after having been denied legal aid. However the US judge ruled against the UK claimants towards the end of 2006. The UK had 'a perfectly appropriate judicial system', argued Merck's counsel. 'In fact, the UK courts are more appropriate than New Jersey because the plaintiffs lived there, they were prescribed their medicine there, they ingested it there, they were treated there, their medical records were there and their physicians lived there.'[14]

The claimant lawyer Martyn Day, senior partner at Leigh Day & Co, took a pessimistic view of the failure of the Vioxx action and what it meant for other product liability litigation. 'I cannot remember the last success there has been in the drugs field,' he said. 'Maybe Myodil during the 1990s, but you could count them on the fingers of one hand.'[15] He was referring to the £7 million settlement in 1995 ending one of the biggest personal injury actions to come before the English courts on behalf of over 400 people against Glaxo claiming back pain was the result of spinal injections of the dye Myodil during back scans.

Vioxx joined a dismal roll call of failed group actions including the 2002 oral contraceptive pill litigation, which dramatically fell apart in 2007 following 44 days of legal argument and the contributions of 10 epidemiologists. Then there was the failed Norplant contraceptive litigation, an abandoned attempt to take on the tobacco companies in 1999, and the notorious benzodiazepine tranquilliser cases, which swallowed up £30 million of taxpayers' money without seeing the inside of a courtroom.

Tight controls have been introduced for complex product liability cases as a result of what the LSC has described as the 'bitter experiences' of cases such as the benzodiazepine tranquilliser fiasco. By direction of the Lord Chancellor, there is only £3 million available for major multiparty actions and litigation is subject to an annual affordability review. In the 2007 affordability review, the LSC was considering funding actions relating to the antidepressant Seroxat; the epilepsy drug sodium valproate; Vigabatrin (Sabril), and other epilepsy treatment; and the osteoarthritic condition known as miners' knee.

The £3 million cap is clearly an issue of access to justice. Drug companies will spend tens, if not hundreds, of millions in research and development alone. Marc Weingarten, the American lawyer who advised the UK Vioxx litigants in the US, made the point that individual expert reports alone can run into 'tens and 20s of thousands of dollars'. What did he make of the £3 million budget available for all UK class actions? 'That is not a lot of money', he replied.[16]

Possible solutions

The idea of the CLAF is one that has periodically surfaced. It was first floated by Justice in 1966, in 1978 and again in 1992 when it called for a pilot with a small amount of funding from the Treasury. In the 1990s, the Law Society, Bar Council and Consumers Association have all backed such a move. The 1978 Royal Commission on Legal Services rejected the idea.

Nevertheless, a CLAF emerged as part of Conservative party policy in the 2001 general election. Under such a scheme, clients would have to pay an application fee in order to discourage frivolous claims and, if successful, claimants would repay a cut, say 10 per cent of damages. The Tories reckoned it would save £300 to £500 million a year from the legal aid budget. However, the Lord Chancellor, Lord Mackay, reckoned that to reach a comprehensive self financing fund it would need to retain about 25 to 30 per cent of damages and charge a fee of £300 when damages were not an issue.

The Civil Justice Council looked at Hong Kong's Supplementary Legal Aid Scheme in 2006. Eligibility for legal aid in Hong Kong is around 20 per cent of the population. The scheme claws back 6 per cent of damages of cases that settle and 12 per cent of those that go to trial. The idea was floated most recently by the Bar Council in 2008. The Bar proposed a 'public/private partnership' model of a CLAF. It explained: 'The principle behind such a fund is that the Legal Services Commission will establish it, or "prime the pump", with sufficient funds to ensure that meritorious qualifying cases can be properly supported and pursued and that the fund is replenished from a small percentage of the damages recovered by successful claimants.'[17]

LAG has acknowledged that there are practical problems with establishing a CLAF, not least how it would co-exist with CFAs. 'There is a risk that the fund may not be big enough unless it takes a disproportionately high slice of the compensation won,' said LAG in 2006. 'And if CFAs are available, the cases with the best chances of success will opt for a CFA, so their compensation remains intact, with the CLAF likely to fund cases with low chances of success. The risk here is that the fund will diminish as it pays the costs of more losing cases than winners.'

Another potential way of helping plug the justice gap is through before-the-event insurance – as opposed to after-the-event policies. In the early 1990s it was floated by the then Lord Chancellor's Department that legal expenses insurance could make up the ground lost as a result of declining eligibility in legal aid.

If there was a compelling argument for it then, that has increased over the years. Most people already have access to free legal advice – albeit in a limited form – through their household and motor insurance policies, trade union membership or other groups such as the AA or RAC. According to a report prepared for the Ministry of

Justice in 2007, almost six out of ten of us have legal expenses insurance (59 per cent).[18] There are six million union members – the benefits offered by union membership tend to be similar in nature to legal expenses insurance.

Policies attached to household insurance are surprisingly wide, usually covering accidents at home or at work and disputes over faulty goods, through to botched building jobs, 'nightmare neighbour' disputes, and employment claims such as unfair dismissal. Typically, a family protection policy might cost £15 to £20 and buy £50,000 worth of protection, which represents good value for money if it delivers what it promises.

The major limitation on bringing access to justice is a practical one. People generally do not know that they have it – according to the Ministry of Justice report less than one in four consumers had even heard of it – and if they do they are not sure what it means. The reason for the low cost of legal expenses insurance is because so many people have it but do not use it. Many people accumulate duplicate and even triplicate cover through various motor, home and travel insurance policies.

The Ministry of Justice report found that legal expenses insurance cover was 'often fragmented', and 'due to lack of awareness' many consumers were oblivious that they had insurance. It called on the Financial Services Authority and Association of British Insurers to agree ways of promoting legal expenses insurance and 'encouraging' policy holders to read their policy documents. It also proposed a change of name 'to something consumers are more likely to understand', such as 'legal protection' and recommended that employers provide legal expenses insurance to employees and housing associations provide it for tenants.

1 *Observer* 27 February 2005.
2 *Independent* 29 March 1991.
3 *Contingency fees* Cm 571, HMSO, 1989.
4 *Legal services: a framework for the future* Cm 740, HMSO, 1989.
5 *Daily Mail* 12 August 1993.
6 *Conditional fee guidance*, Bar Council, 2006.
7 Lord Irvine of Lairg, speech to Law Society's annual conference, 18 October 1997.
8 *New Statesman* 31 October 1997.
9 *Law Society Gazette* 17 July 2008.
10 Stella Yarrow and Pamela Abrams, *Nothing to lose?*, University of Westminster, 1999.

11 James Sandbach, *No win, no fee, no chance*, Citizens Advice, 2004 p2.
12 *Observer* 24 December 2006.
13 Ministry of Justice research conducted by Professors Richard Moorhead, Paul Fenn and Neil Rickman, publication due 2009.
14 *Independent Lawyer* March 2007.
15 *Independent Lawyer* November 2006.
16 *Independent Lawyer* November 2006.
17 Discussion paper, *Legal aid and the public interest*, Bar Council, May 2008, p16.
18 *The market for 'BTE' legal expenses insurance*, Ministry of Justice, July 2007.

CHAPTER 8

Crime: supplier-induced demand

'It is perhaps the biggest miscarriage of justice in today's system when the guilty walk away unpunished.' So said Tony Blair, when Prime Minister, at a conference of police officers and criminal justice experts from the UK and America in June 2002. In the same speech he promised to 'rebalance' our criminal justice system and proposed to scrap the 800-year-old double jeopardy rule preventing people being tried who had already been acquitted of an offence.

At the time of going to press there have been over 60 pieces of criminal justice legislation introduced by New Labour. A government with such a radical approach to criminal justice would be unlikely to shirk from sorting out the public funding of criminal defence work. A month after Blair's 'rebalancing' speech, Lord Carter was invited to conduct his 'procurement' review charged with the job of containing a growing criminal budget.

To begin with, New Labour's reforming zeal was primarily for the civil scheme and the establishment of a Community Legal Service (CLS). As explained in Chapter 5, New Labour's vision for the CLS was positive (delivering a comprehensive service matching provision with local need) whereas its vision for a Criminal Defence Service (CDS) was, to be generous, driven by a desire to rationalise an administratively chaotic profession. It is telling that no mention of a CDS (or criminal legal aid for that matter) was contained in New Labour's manifesto, unlike the CLS.

The government's take on criminal defence legal aid was of a system losing money like bad plumbing leaking water. It urgently needed to be fixed. The rising cost of civil legal aid (from £544 million in 1994 to £634 million in 1998) was easily outstripped by criminal legal aid rising from £666 million in 1994 to £892 million in 1998. The criminal spend was about to take off, though, as a result of New Labour's promise to be 'tough on crime and tough on the causes of crime'.

To provide an overview of New Labour's approach to the public funding of criminal defence, under Lord Irvine's watch, the Legal Aid Board (LAB) – and then the Legal Services Commission (LSC) – set about tinkering with the system trying to find those leaks. The big gusher was those very high cost cases (the 2 per cent in terms of total volume of cases that came to consume 90 per cent of the budget).

Under Lord Falconer, patience quickly ran out. One of the government's favourite troubleshooters, Lord Carter of Coles, was quickly dispatched with a very large hammer to tend to the problem. However, publicly-funded criminal defence work is complex and multifaceted. There proved no easy way to turn off the high cost case pipeline, and so Lord Carter scratched his head for a while. Then the LSC pretty much returned to tinkering.

Cutting out the cowboys

In 1998 there were 1,282 firms with criminal legal aid franchises but more than 5,000 firms doing criminal work. According to the LAB, six out of ten firms receiving criminal legal aid payments (excluding Crown Court) earned less than £20,000 a year. The criminal defence profession was a cottage industry handled largely by small high street practices (as it remains to this day).

In Lord Irvine's Cardiff speech in 1997 at the Law Society's annual conference, the Lord Chancellor was largely quiet on his vision for a criminal defence profession.[1] 'In the medium term, the greater part of criminal work will be drawn into contracting arrangements,' he said. 'But we will need to work hard to decide how the interests of justice in criminal cases – particularly the rights of defendants and the need to avoid delay – can be dovetailed with a contracting system managed through the LAB.' That work he assured delegates was 'already in hand'.

Fundamental reform was already underway as a result of Lord Mackay's Lord Chancellorship under the previous Conservative administration. At the time of the Cardiff speech, plans for a pilot of 'block contracting' – where firms would be paid a fixed fee for conducting all of the work in a certain area – were in place for police station advice work and court duty work. There was a split between the high street firms and the small number of larger practices which backed reforms anticipating that they would do well out of the economies of scale.

Only franchised solicitors would be able to apply for legal aid crime contracts in 2000. The vision of a post-reform criminal defence profession was hazy if not absent. Just what shape would contracting leave the criminal defence profession in? Observers were estimating anywhere between '250 up to 1,000' firms would be left.[2] Steve Orchard, LAB's chief executive, in characteristically bullish form, dismissed concerns about contracting reducing professional independence as 'a complete red herring'. 'The profession is terrified of the thought of contracting because it's different,' he said. 'Anyone can do legal aid now. Contracting will stop that. It will concentrate work on firms and reward them appropriately for doing that – and it will cut out the cowboys.' In November 1998 Lord Irvine, giving evidence before a House of Commons' home affairs committee, said that all criminal defence services would be brought under contract by 2003.

Modernising justice

The vision for the CDS was laid out in December 1998's *Modernising justice* white paper.[3] The cost-cutting agenda was to the fore. Criminal legal aid was 'rising at an alarming rate', a 44 per cent increase between 1992/93 (£507 million) and 1997/98 (£733 million). Over the same period, the number of criminal legal aid orders for representation at court rose by only 10 per cent, from 563,788 to 618,621. The position was 'worst' in the higher criminal courts ('the single most expensive element of the criminal legal aid system') where spending had risen 58 per cent in that period, from £221 million to £349 million, while the number of cases remained constant at 124,000.

The framework for determining lawyers' rates of pay was 'inflexible and outdated'. Standard fees introduced by Lord Mackay in 1995, the first time a government had departed from hourly rates in the criminal field, had increased control over expenditure.

Lawyers were to blame for rising costs and were accused of maximising their bills and stringing out the work. They were placed under 'inappropriate financial incentives' and adjournments were sought unnecessarily, guilty pleas delayed until the last moment, and cases taken to the Crown Court unnecessarily.

The big problem identified in *Modernising justice* was, inevitably, the gusher – those very expensive cases (that were to become known as the very high cost criminal cases or VHCCs) devouring an increasingly disproportionate share of the budget. In 1996/97, 42 per cent of legal aid spending in the Crown Court (almost £116 million) was on just 1,000 (1 per cent) of the cases. The solution was to build on Lord Mackay's franchising, replacing the existing criminal legal aid scheme with the new CDS. The paper also proposed separating the criminal budget from the CLS budget. 'Separating the two schemes in this way reflects the fact that they are responsible for providing different types of service in very different types of case,' the white paper noted.

The CDS would be provided by private practice under contracts. Contract prices would be fixed ('fixed prices create an incentive to keep delay to a minimum') and firms would cover the full range from police station to Crown Court ('[to] eliminate the fragmentation that bedevils the current scheme'). The most expensive cases, defined as where the trial was expected to last 25 days or more, would be dealt with under separate contracts negotiated for each case. The defendant's choice of solicitor would be restricted to firms on a specialist panel. This approach would enable the CDS to 'keep a tight rein on the cost of potentially long, complex and expensive criminal cases, rather than handing over a blank cheque'.

Contracting 'inevitably' involved restriction on 'the unfettered choice of lawyer that clients have', the white paper noted, but ministers judged that to be 'necessary and desirable in order to secure quality and value for money'. But choice was important because competition improved quality and 'lawyers who rely for future business on being chosen are likely to pursue their clients' interests robustly'. Competition was also important to secure better value for the taxpayer's money and it was proposed that firms should bid for work available anticipating the introduction of competitive tendering. '[Firms] would be awarded more or fewer duty solicitor "slots", on the basis of the prices they offered, both for that work and for any subsequent representation at court. The more firms acted as duty solicitors, the more clients they would tend to attract, so earning more money in total.'

It also included proposals to drop the 'complex and costly' process of means testing – less than 1 per cent of applicants were refused criminal legal aid because they had sufficient means to pay for their own defence. The total value of contributions collected was 'barely enough to pay for running the means testing system'. It was proposed in the Crown Court only to grant the judge the power to order a defendant to pay some or all costs.

Another controversial innovation was to be the establishment of a Public Defender Service (PDS). 'Evidence from other countries suggests that properly funded salaried defenders can be more cost-effective and provide a better service than lawyers in private practice,' the paper said. The report referenced a trial pilot north of the border in Scotland. That scheme was getting off to a rocky start. Baroness Helena Kennedy QC was critical of the Scottish scheme, calling it 'justice by star sign' after the pilot relied upon suspects born in two particular months being compelled to be represented by the office. The PDS would also provide an alternative to private practice if gaps appeared in coverage.

Access to justice

Most of the proposals were incorporated into the Access to Justice Bill, which received royal assent in July 1999. There was a slow dawning of realisation that the overall cap for the legal aid budget would lead to the civil budget being eaten away by the criminal spend. Due to the Human Rights Act 1998, funding for representation in criminal cases is a priority whereas much of the civil budget, especially legal help and certificated social welfare law, is in reality discretionary. 'The effect of this is that, if the cost of criminal legal aid continues to increase at anything like its present rate, spending on civil legal aid will be steadily squeezed out of existence,' reflected Lord Goodhart QC, the Liberal Democrat spokesman on legal affairs in the House of Lords in 1999. 'If spending on legal aid had been capped in 1994, but spending on criminal legal aid had subsequently remained at its actual figures, I estimate that (allowing for an annual increase in the cap at or a little above the rate of inflation) spending on civil legal aid would by 1998 have had to be cut by at least £100 million (as compared with 1994) in real terms. It would not take many years of this to wipe out civil legal aid altogether, with all the consequences that would have for the protection of the rights of ordinary people.' The government's failure to link criminal legal aid to the wider criminal justice system, especially when it was determined to increase the number of people going through it, was bad enough – but even worse was linking it to the fate of the civil legal aid scheme.

The start date for contracting for criminal defence firms was April 2001. Before the launch of the CDS there were 3,500 firms offering criminal representation – just over 500 firms dropped out. Most of those that went were the dabblers, undertaking little defence work, and their disappearance had little impact in terms of service.

In the run-up to the introduction of contracting, there was a notable deterioration in the relationship between ministers and a profession unhappy with the perceived one-sided nature of contract negotiations and antagonised by an eight-year pay freeze. Civil practitioners had that year received a 10 per cent increase. The reason for that, as explained by the LSC, was that civil spend was under control but criminal was rocketing. The costs of the magistrates' court work had gone up by 25 per cent to £125 million in four years and Crown Court by 40 per cent to £158 million. It was reported that 1 per cent of the cases accounted for 49 per cent of legal aid expenditure in the Crown Court. The reason for the increase in the magistrates' courts work was a huge jump in the number of representation orders, up by 35 per cent in one year alone. This was caused by the changes in the system brought in by the Narey proposals to speed up the administration of the criminal justice system. In January 2002 there was to be the first in a damaging series of stand-offs between the profession and the LSC when more than 60 criminal specialist firms (including Christian Fisher, Bindman & Partners, Fisher Meredith and Hodge Jones & Allen) backed a declaration of support from the Law Society that contracts should not be signed until they were deemed 'fair and workable and the rates of remuneration were fair and reasonable'. There was also internal frustration within the profession and its representative groups over whether it was possible in a climate of a growing spend on criminal work to resist reforms. As Angus Andrew, chair of the Law Society's representation committee (and soon to be LSC commissioner) noted, with a £1.7 billion spend on legal aid, arguing for an increase in scope, eligibility and legal aid rates appeared 'increasingly futile'.[4] At a Law Society Council meeting he described Chancery Lane's policy as tantamount to 'wanting to die in a ditch'.

'BMW-driving civil liberties lawyers'

Intransigence on the part of the profession was matched by an absence of sympathy or even understanding on the part of the government of the role of defence lawyers in society. There were some crude bouts of lawyer-bashing. In early 2001 Jack Straw, the then Home Secretary, provocatively and inaccurately claimed that lawyers would soon outnumber police officers and that the only thing they could ever agree about was 'taking money off clients'. Straw, a lawyer, lambasted 'very aggressive defence lawyers' who 'sometimes forget about their wider social responsibilities and their responsibilities to the court, and in trying to protect their niche markets with the local criminal fraternity act in a way which would have been unacceptable when I was practising 25 years ago'. The Home Secretary was responding to what he saw as a failure to take up his newly introduced anti-social behaviour orders but was, no doubt, mindful of wider problems in the profession. He had previously accused 'BMW-driving civil liberties lawyers' for opposition to his anti-social behaviour orders (ASBOs).[5]

Roy Amlot, Bar Council chairman, accused the Home Secretary of betraying 'a dangerous reactionary attitude towards the criminal justice system'. 'The Home Secretary's dark and disturbing sentiments place too much emphasis on obtaining convictions regardless of their safety,' he said. The Law Society flagged up a factual inaccuracy that there were only 11,300 solicitors doing criminal work compared with 125,000 police officers.

Shortly after the exchange almost 1,000 of those defence lawyers met in London and according to one report 'all but eight' backed a motion not to sign up to the contract. However, having climbed to the top of the hill, a couple of weeks before the deadline the Law Society told members to trudge back down and sign up. In July that year it was reported that 2,894 firms signed up to a contracting regime worth a total of £39.4 million. There were to be more ill-tempered stand-offs (for example, at the end of 2003 when the LSC issued notices to terminate all legal aid contracts from 2004 to make way for amendments to the standard terms and, in 2007, when there was a near total breakdown of relations over the introduction of a 'unified' contract).

Solidarity was to prove an elusive concept within the disparate community of criminal defence solicitors. There was always the suspicion that firms would break ranks. The Bar was to prove rather more effective at industrial action – although it has been very careful to make the point that any action taken by its members was taken in their individual capacity (for fear of government retaliation under competition law).

Another source of antagonism between private practice and the government was the fledgling Public Defender Service. The first offices opened in 2001 in Liverpool, Birmingham, Middlesbrough and Swansea (Cheltenham and Pontypridd were to launch in 2002). They were regarded as a thinly-veiled threat by the defence profession – 'if you don't co-operate then we'll bring you in-house and put you on a salary'. Many defence lawyers expressed their objection to the PDS in terms of the erosion of professional independence but it was a lightning rod for other grievances within the profession. The LSC allocated a first-year budget of up to £3 million for start-up and running costs of six public defender offices. That money came out of the overall annual criminal legal aid budget. 'The state arrests, prosecutes and sentences individuals involved in the criminal justice system,' the Criminal Law Solicitors Association argued in 2001. 'For the state to purport to defend that individual will allow a breeding ground for miscarriages of justice.'

It is debatable as to whether a defence profession held under short-leash contracts and existing, according to some practitioners, on the brink of bankruptcy is going to be more independent-minded than the salaried defence lawyer.

Putting aside the ethical arguments over public defenders' independence, it quickly became apparent that a PDS would be less economical than private practice. The Public Defence Solicitors Office in Scotland, two years into its own pilot project at the time of the launch of the service south of the border, was costing £360 per case compared to £290 for private practice. In 2007, the LSC came to much the same conclusion when a report by Lee Bridges and Avrom Sherr found that the running costs of the PDS offices were 41 to 93 per cent higher than in private practice.[6] 'I would improve my service if I got a 93 per cent increase in pay. I'd turn up to court in a Lamborghini for a start,' quipped defence lawyer Andrew Keogh.[7] A fundamental problem with the PDS is that it flies in the face of the criminal law practice model. Criminal law specialists develop their practices by establishing a following of clients through their work in the magistrates' court and police station. Generally, when new practices open solicitors have to bring existing clients with them. The PDS services were starting from nothing (hence the element of coercion in the Scottish service).

After the Bridges/Sherr report, ministers initially defended the service. The then legal aid minister Vera Baird QC said that the research showed 'very clearly that the PDS is independent and gives robust advice'. 'The PDS has a future,' she declared. Within a few weeks, the government announced that 18 lawyers and advisers working in the PDS would be pursuing their futures elsewhere. It closed down the Birmingham, Chester and Liverpool offices and decided not to reopen Middlesbrough. Its role has now been reduced to the Green Goddess of the criminal justice system, a skeleton service kept on standby if market forces fail under the Carter reforms.

Turf war

The outgoing chief executive of the LSC, Steve Orchard, has admitted to tension between the Treasury and the LCD. 'Things have got to be proven from a blank sheet of paper, which I do find frustrating because some of us actually know quite a lot and have examined most of the issues that they want to examine afresh,' Orchard said.[8] The 'worst-case scenario' would be 'massively increasing spends on criminal defence' eating into the CLS, he warned.

In June 2003 the government continued its programme of reforms – extending individual case contracts to cover all high cost criminal cases (over £150,000 or lasting more than 25 days at trial); reducing free police station advice; seeking to confine the interests of justice test to cover mainly cases where imprisonment was the likely sentence; removing the right to standalone advice and assistance for people facing criminal investigations where the interest of justice test is not satisfied (excluding cases such as motoring offences where the penalty is a fine); restricting the court duty solicitor scheme; and imposing a tougher system for recouping legal aid payments from those who are convicted.[9]

When Lord Irvine left the office of Lord Chancellor in 2003, critics complained that the Treasury had won out in the internecine battle. 'Sadly his epitaph will not be as a reformer who introduced the CLS but as a Lord Chancellor who was outmanoeuvred by the Home Office and the Treasury and failed to secure the budgetary increases his department needed,' commented the Legal Aid Practitioners Group. There was talk of a division between Irvine and then Home Secretary David Blunkett over the latter's policies eating into the legal aid budget. It was even rumoured that he considered resigning over the issue at one point. However, the dismissal by one commentator that 'a man with an ego the size of France' would never take such a step has a ring of truth.[10]

It is hard not to resist the conclusion that much of the government's time spent analysing cost savings in the criminal legal aid budget has been spent looking down the wrong end of the telescope. The convenient conclusion settled upon by the government was that the greatest culprits in the criminal justice system were the defendants and their unscrupulous lawyers playing the system. Ministers developed an almost pathological refusal to accept that New Labour's relentless lawmaking could contribute to pressures on the courts when people were brought to book in increasing numbers. Blunkett, like his predecessor Home Secretary Jack Straw, blamed the 'adjournment culture' among defence lawyers for much of what he reckoned to be £80 million wasted on trials that did not go ahead – despite the fact that his own department told a more complicated story. A Home Office study found that just over one-fifth (20.6 per cent) of adjournments in magistrates' courts were because the defence was not ready and roughly the same number (19.8 per cent) were caused by the Crown Prosecution Service (CPS) not being ready.[11]

Similarly, the Audit Commission undermined claims that delays were mostly the fault of the defence. Between April 2001 and January 2002, 15 per cent of ineffective Crown Court trials were caused by the defence not being ready and 11 per cent by the prosecution needing more time.[12]

Lord Irvine, to his credit, did not appear to buy into the myopic New Labour analysis. 'The major factor in offenders not being brought to justice was that of every 100 crimes recorded by the police, only about 24 are successfully detected,' Lord Irvine reflected in 2002. 'The police take action in 19, of which four are discontinued or written off by the CPS, five result in cautions, nine result in guilty pleas or convictions after trial – and just one result in an acquittal.'

Nor did the LSC (or at least its researchers) take the government line. A study by Professor Ed Cape at the University of the West of England and Professor Richard Moorhead at Cardiff Law School explicitly blamed government policy and prosecution practice for rising legal aid costs.[13] Cape and Moorhead said it was 'irresponsible' for the government to lay the blame for increases in legal aid at 'the profession's door' because the key factor was the number of people who were being 'processed' by the criminal justice system. The report explicitly rejected the government contention that there was 'a supplier induced demand' – in other words, that lawyers were managing their work to maximise income thus fuelling the increases in legal aid costs. Cape and Moorhead argued that 'supplier-induced demand' was a 'rather value-laden concept' and that the problem was in fact the reverse.

Their report was an important document. It articulated what should have been a rather obvious truth that pressure on costs was being caused by a number of factors. Not least that there were more cases being prosecuted, more defendants imprisoned, plus there was the deployment of new technology such as DNA testing and CCTV as well as changes in criminal proceedings which increased the work which needed to be carried out.

'The Ministry of Justice are no nearer getting to grips with the causes of why criminal legal aid expenditure has grown,' said Cape.

The academic did offer some pointers as to likely factors. 'The greater use of imprisonment will lead to more expenditure on criminal legal aid as the likelihood of loss of liberty is the most common reason for the grant of legal aid. We are also seeing the numbers of arrests creeping up resulting in a greater need for advice.'

Since coming to power the Labour government has increased expenditure on policing by 40 per cent in real terms, boosting the numbers of police officers by 14,233.[14] 'You would expect an increase in policing to lead to more arrests and convictions, unless they are spending the money for nothing,' said Cape.

The Cape/Moorhead report should have kicked into touch that idea that controlling costs by squeezing lawyers was sufficient to control the legal aid budget.

Planning blight

There was no danger of Lord Irvine's successor, Lord Falconer, being 'outmanoeuvred' by the Home Office. His consistent view was that the criminal spend was a problem generated by legal aid lawyers. As predicted, a rather contrived crisis began to emerge: how could the growing criminal legal aid budget be controlled to prevent 'the death of civil legal aid'?

New proposals came out of the LSC at the start of 2004. The LSC would take much more 'command control' of the defence profession. In particular, it announced plans to reduce the number of criminal contract holders by as much as two-thirds and London firms were set to be reduced by at least half. The solution was a response to a polarised defence market where the big conurbations were over-populated and rural areas under-served. In London and the big cities, the LSC would cut back and firms would bid for contracts. Where there were shortages, the LSC would offer a package of incentives such as grants, soft loans, and guaranteed income to encourage newcomers. The idea of a roving PDS was also raised where lawyers could be parachuted into private practice firms. Firms would compete on price in oversubscribed areas and so this was an end to the 'one size fits all' criminal defence contract and the introduction of price competitive tendering.

The LSC also proposed the introduction of CDS Direct which, like NHS Direct, would provide an initial diagnostic service to police stations. Defence solicitors would only be contacted if legal advice in person was actually needed. There was finally some recognition of the pressures on legal aid from other areas of the criminal justice system. For the first time, the LSC was to measure the cost of proposed changes to the criminal justice system in advance and then relevant government departments such as the Home Office would be responsible for footing the bill through the legal aid impact test.

There appears to be considerable confusion about the rationale behind the scheme. In June 2007 it was revealed that less than £2 million had been paid into the legal aid fund – comprising just two sums of £35,000 from the Department for Environment, Food and Rural Affairs and £1.9 million from the Department for Education and Skills. Not a penny from the Home Office had been forthcoming. A spokesman from the Ministry of Justice attempted to clarify the point. 'It is wrong to say the test is not working,' she said.[15] 'It has been extremely successful in its purpose which is to check legal aid costs are consistently identified when new policies are developed by government.' She went on to say that the test was 'not intended as a mechanism for collecting additional funding from other government departments' but to provide 'the opportunities to suggest changes to policy owners in order to minimise the financial impact of policy'. It was a surprising assertion and suggested a retreat on what could have been a very useful scheme.

The 2004 paper also proposed the reintroduction of a simplified means test – the same means test that was cancelled on the basis that it cost more than it saved only a few years ago. Its reintroduction indicated a rather hopeful approach to belt-tightening. It also suggested a populist approach from a government keen to address the damage of press stories about £40,000-a-week football stars being allowed public funds for allegedly spitting on fans (as in the case of the Bolton Wanderers' striker El Hadji Diouf) or Lotto multimillionaires being granted legal aid to defend themselves against charges of affray (as in the case of Michael Carroll). In the cash-strapped world of legal aid, it might seem hard to object to the 'can pay, should pay' principle that the return of the means test represented. However, LAG has concerns about 2008 consultations looking to extend the means test to the Crown Court and limit the recovery of costs for those acquitted (see later). The reintroduction of the means test in the magistrates' court was to push defence solicitors once again to the brink as they were expected to bear the cost of administering the scheme (previously they had been paid under the old green form scheme for checking out welfare benefit entitlements and chasing pay slips).

Bar wars

Meanwhile there was trouble brewing at the publicly funded Bar, incensed at the government refusal to increase graduated fees since they were introduced in 1997 and plans to extend contracts to all high cost criminal cases from April 2004. Defence counsel would have to agree all work in advance with LSC contract managers. Such micromanagement of cases went down badly with the independent Bar. One silk complained of having to argue 'that an average of three minutes per page to read complicated statements was "reasonable"'.[16] 'At one point, my manager tried to persuade me that 15 seconds per page of exhibits was all that was required,' he said. It was also reported that an LSC contracts manager had claimed there was no need for leading counsel to read through a statement if it had already been seen by the solicitor or junior counsel because they could write a summary.

The Bar had no reservations when it came to 'downing wigs'. 'Once the leading criminal defence barristers realised what the Government was up to, they formed a committee at the end of last year which now represents 50 sets of chambers. Last month, it agreed a policy of simply refusing to take on any more VHCCs,' the *Daily Telegraph* reported. As a result, it was impossible in many parts of England and Wales 'for solicitors to find a barrister prepared to take on complex murders, heavy frauds and other major cases', the paper said. There was a similar outbreak of industrial action in 2008 over pay rates for VHCCs when only three Queen's Counsel signed up to the LSC panel. Under the scheme, rates started at £70 an hour for a junior barrister and £91 for a QC. It was reckoned that at least five VHCCs (including the high profile murder trial of 11-year-old Rhys Jones) might be affected by the boycott.

There was not much solidarity within the wider profession, though. Many solicitors felt with some justification that the Bar had largely escaped the pay freeze they had endured for ten years. In the 2004 stand-off ministers managed to find £17 million despite their protestations that no money was available, a sum that the Law Centre Federation reflected would be enough to set up 65 new law centres and pay their running costs for a year. Richard Miller, director of the Legal Aid Practitioners' Group, argued that it would be a 'major setback if the Government were to capitulate at the first complaint' when 'moderate voices within the solicitors' profession' had argued that damaging the interests of clients was 'not the way to maintain remuneration rates at an adequate level'. There were plenty of less moderate voices among solicitors, though, who felt frustrated that the profession could not get its act together.

By the start of summer 2004, the Bar had secured the £17 million package in extra fees (£6 million for graduated fees plus an £11 million for VHCCs). How did the Bar deliver where the solicitors' profession failed? 'If you get QCs dropping out of big cases on the front pages of the newspapers immediately before an election, you get politicians hurting where it hurts most,' commented one LSC insider. 'The Bar might be smooth gentlemen. But when it comes to a punch up they are much better than the Law Society.'

In the middle of that rather fraught period between the profession and the government, the then legal aid Minister David Lammy announced what was grandly called the fundamental legal aid review (FLAR). It was to be the first time any government had stepped back and asked the question: what is legal aid for? The fact that a review was taking place when ministers had so firmly indicated their intention to slash criminal defence spending appeared disingenuous. Nevertheless a floor was cleared at the Lord Chancellor's Department and the FLAR began.

The start of the FLAR in 2004 marked the beginning of a three-year period of 'planning blight'. A few ideas were to slip through the self-imposed purdah, such as the preferred supplier scheme and a consultation on competitive tendering, but the reform programme was put on hold. The results of the FLAR were never made public. Instead the government published *A fairer deal for legal aid* in July 2005, recommending tighter management of larger and complex cases, such as murder and fraud, and cutting the spend on VHCCs; and a review of procurement by Lord Carter.[17]

That paper again focused on rising costs and reported that 'half of all legal aid spending in the Crown Court goes on just 1% of cases', that 13 cases alone cost £48 million, and that criminal legal aid costs had risen overall by 37 per cent in real terms in seven years. By contrast, spending on civil and family legal aid (excluding asylum) had fallen by 24 per cent during the same period. 'The disproportionate amount of money spent on defending high cost criminal cases must be redistributed to help ensure all criminal cases are dealt with swiftly and fairly,' Lord Falconer said.

It noted that the cost of the criminal justice system had shot up by over 46 per cent since 1998/99 in real terms, driven by 'government policy to tackle persistent offending and antisocial behaviour and to increase the number of offenders brought to justice'.

Did this have any impact on legal aid? Apparently not. 'There is no demonstrable link that increased spending on the CJS has directly translated into increased volumes of work' either in terms of police station advice, representation in magistrates' courts or in the Crown Court.

Shortly after *A fairer deal* was published, it was reported that the 'legal aid crisis' was 'much deeper' than Lord Falconer had suggested in the press briefings announcing the paper. A black hole was emerging in the finances of the Department for Constitutional Affairs. 'What reporters were not told was that, on present projections, the legal aid budget will overspend by £130 million this year and by similar amounts in subsequent years,' it was reported.[18] In that context, Lord Falconer's pledge to introduce immediate measures 'to save £7 million this year and more next year in the most expensive cases' would have 'as much impact on the £130 million shortfall as a space probe hitting a comet'. His plan was to halve the differential between senior lawyers and junior lawyers in longer cases by reducing the 'gradient' in cases lasting longer than ten days and by reducing the enhancements that courts award solicitors in exceptionally demanding cases – a move that upset the Bar.

Get Carter

A fairer deal announced Lord Carter's review of procurement. It seemed that Lord Falconer lost patience with the LSC's tinkering. 'Lord Carter will produce a plan to produce modern procurement methods to contribute to a more proportionate way of spending legal aid while ensuring reasonable client choice and sufficient quality,' Lord Falconer said. 'The review is an opportunity to correct any anomalies in the current payment system.'

Around this time the LSC was noticeably brought closer to government. The senior civil servant Derek Hill left the Lord Chancellor's Department (where he was involved with the FLAR) to join the LSC to head up the CDS. Michael Bichard came on board as the new chair of the LSC and one of the first things that arrived on his desk was the Carter review. He had previously worked with David Blunkett (as permanent secretary at the Department of Education and Employment and chaired the Soham murders enquiry). The LSC was a very different body to the one run by Steve Orchard.

Lord Carter of Coles delivered his report for a market-based legal system in February 2006 after a year-long inquiry. For a businessman, who had already chaired reviews into fraught and complex issues such as the Commonwealth Games 2002 and the Wembley Stadium, sorting out a relative backwater of public expenditure such as criminal legal aid must have seemed uncontroversial.

At the launch, Lord Carter pointed out that since 1997 spending on criminal legal aid had risen by 37 per cent in real terms from £730 million to nearly £1.2 billion. 'We should be proud of our system of criminal legal aid,' he said. 'It ensures that everyone, whatever their wealth, has access to justice. But there are inherent inefficiencies in the way that criminal legal aid work is procured and that needs addressing if we are to control increasing costs.'

The original Carter blueprint had 62 recommendations, notably: best value tendering (BVT) for legal aid contracts from 2009; that contracts should no longer be awarded to firms earning less than £50,000; fixed fees in police stations (including waiting and travelling times); revised graduated fees for Crown Court advocates and litigators by April 2007; a new graduated fee scheme in the magistrates' courts by April 2008; and tighter control of VHCCs.[19]

Initial responses to the Carter report from the criminal solicitors' groups were predictably hostile – 'ill considered', 'unresearched', 'likely to be a disaster' and to 'destroy the criminal justice system'. Many defence lawyers rejected the need for the review right from the start. The Criminal Law Solicitors Association's submission, for example, rejected 'very emphatically' the need to reform procurement.

In fact, many longer standing staff at the LSC were unhappy at having an external review foisted upon them. Tony Edwards, the former Legal Services Commissioner in charge of the defence portfolio for seven years from 2000, acknowledged that the Carter review was sprung upon the LSC as much as it was upon the profession. He argued that Carter derailed the good work of the LSC and also described 'every single detail of Carter' as 'wrong'. 'We could have achieved everything that the Government wanted if we just went a little more slowly, took out the small players, not allowed any new contracts – that's all you need to do – and over five years the market would reform itself,' he said.[20]

Lord Carter believed such a negative response from the profession was effectively 'giving themselves up as a hostage to fortune'. 'Everybody knows the system needs reforming. To say nothing needs changing is, dare I say it, a bit Luddite.'[21] When asked how lawyers differed from the subject of his other reviews, Carter replied that the issue of 'supplier interest' had never been quite so 'dominant' as it was with the legal aid profession. He also complained to the press at the time of 'whining' lawyers and eradicating the 'whinge factor'.

Carter was said to have found a service 'that, if not quite dying, was time-limited because of the average age of practitioners – many in their fifties – and demoralised, with unfairnesses in the way that practitioners are paid'.[22] 'I was quite shocked, in certain parts, by the clear impoverishment of it. You do have incredible inequities in the system, some people do well and others doing not very well at all. And there is a general sense of unhappiness.'

Carter was quick to clarify that he was not proposing a system defined by untrammelled market forces. In his first public meeting, he said: 'One of the fears was that we might just want unbridled competition simply based on price. It is something that we aren't prepared to let happen because we believe that quality is central.' Minimum quality standards would be tested through peer review and the responsibility for that would eventually pass to the Law Society. He denied that 'thousands' of firms would be axed although he pointed out that more than 2,500 firms were undertaking criminal legal work and of those 400 did less than a combined total of £7 million. 'I can't believe that they survive on £16,000 of legal aid', he said; indicating that such firms would either merge or shut.

Lord Carter rejected arguments that his proposals prejudiced independent-minded defence lawyers who would fight harder for their clients and therefore have higher bids reflecting higher costs. When asked about this, Carter replied brusquely: 'The idea that this is some part of a political plot to benefit the prosecution and in some way shift the legal process is incorrect.' But the point was more subtle – not necessarily a 'political plot', rather a politically convenient oversight.

The combined impact of an administratively messy reintroduction of means testing and the Carter review prompted another attempt by solicitors to strike. A new group, the Criminal Defence Solicitors Union, was formed as defence lawyers ran out of patience with the Law Society and other representative bodies. This development happened as Chancery Lane was pushing legal aid up the agenda as a result of the arrival of a new chief executive, Desmond Hudson, and the Liverpool legal aid lawyer Andrew Holroyd who became Law Society president.

In this rather febrile atmosphere, both the profession and the LSC began upping the ante. The LSC announced its timetable for the Carter revolution, bringing forward competitive tendering for crime by a year to October 2008.[23] Fixed fees in police station work were pencilled in for October 2007, revised standard fees in the magistrates' courts and revised graduated fee scheme for advocates from April 2007, litigators' graduated fees scheme from October 2007 for Crown Court outside the VHCC regime, and by October 2008 a single graduated fee scheme for both litigators and advocates.

The Carter consultation prompted 2,325 responses which the Department for Constitutional Affairs admitted were 'largely negative' in tone. 'Many respondents anticipated that they and many of their colleagues would see a drop in income and that this would cause them to re-evaluate whether to continue with publicly funded work,' it blandly stated.[24] Lord Falconer acknowledged concerns but warned practitioners 'to knuckle down and work out how it will work in practice because what we are talking about is delivering for the client'.

The House of Commons' constitutional affairs committee echoed practitioner concerns in April 2006. In their report, the MPs quoted Professor Ed Cape who argued that implementing Carter without piloting its proposals was 'reckless' on the grounds that the changes would be 'irreversible'. The academic unfavourably compared the proposed introduction of the Carter reforms with the introduction of contracting back in 2001 when the LAB piloted the scheme over two to three years. 'If it results in large-scale damage to the legal profession there is no coming back from that other than over a lengthy period of time,' he said. 'You would have lost all the legal aid lawyers.'

Post Carter

The implementation of Carter has been a complex process, sometimes honouring the spirit of its architect and sometimes not. The LSC finally unveiled its blueprint for BVT at the end of 2007 with roll-out at the earliest in 2009. 'We think we have got the best legal aid system in the world,' said Sir Michael Bichard, the then chair of the LSC announcing the publication of *Best value tendering of criminal defence services*.[25] 'It is also the most expensive system in the world and it does not always provide consistent quality or accessibility across the country.' The concept was straightforward. Solicitors would bid for quantities of work, making their bids predicated on the fee level at which they would be willing to do the work. Carter insisted that firms would not just win on the basis of lowest price because firms would have to meet quality criteria monitored by peer review.

The main reason for BVT was described in that paper thus: '... [the] current system provides no mechanism to demonstrate objectively that the Commission is paying sufficient amounts to ensure a sustainable and quality service, but no more than is necessary to ensure best value for the taxpayer.'

BVT was introduced in April 2000 by New Labour with the promise to transform our town hall services and to replace compulsory competitive tendering which required local government to parcel up services into tenders which were then subject to competitive bids. Compulsory competitive tendering was unpopular with both contractors and local authorities. The former resented submitting tenders to what were often hostile clients and councils disliked government meddling with their freedom to decide how to provide local services. Under BVT it was no longer compulsory for local councils to put out their services to compulsory competition with the private sector. Instead local authorities were required to 'make arrangements to secure continuous improvement in the way in which its functions are exercised, having regard to a combination of economy, efficiency and effectiveness'. Local authorities therefore could choose whether or not to offer tenders, but they would also have to justify their decision within the principles of best value.

The criminal defence profession is not like local government. The criminal legal aid market has a single buyer (the LSC) and many sellers. Economists call this situation a 'monopsonistic' market. In a monopsony a buyer can control the market by setting prices and volumes of work. By introducing fixed fees the LSC has set prices and will attempt to control the volume of work by specifying the amount of work for which firms should tender. Controlling volumes of criminal work is problematic because they are determined by factors largely beyond the control of the LSC and firms. It can be argued that fixing fees in such a market can work so long as the buyer, the LSC, does not squeeze down too hard on costs by setting rates below an economically sustainable level. This might lead to short-term savings, but in the long term firms would leave the market and not be replaced, leading to fewer services.

It has been argued that BVT will not work in criminal defence because the LSC cannot guarantee the volume of work offered to firms. 'Firms will bid for the work at the price the LSC sets because they are desperate for work, but the LSC is selling something it does not have at a price it says it cannot afford,' commented Rodney Warren, director of the Criminal Law Solicitors Association. If the LSC gets it wrong and the bids simply go to the lowest bidder, not only does the LSC get a service that the chosen firm cannot deliver but the competition goes out of business.

The introduction of BVT represents a major challenge not only to the profession but to the LSC. Running a tendering system is not without its costs and between 5 to 10 per cent of the total cost of a public service can be absorbed by the procurement process. The LSC plans to do this at a time when it is seeking to reduce its own administrative costs and could risk organisational meltdown in the process.

Much of the evidence concerning the contracting for criminal legal aid services in North America indicates that there are reductions in quality and the creation of cartels which lead to an increase in costs. For example, in San Diego criminal defence service costs rose by 65 per cent after the introduction of competitive bidding.[26] The American Bar Association has also highlighted the increases in prices and concerns over quality which have followed the introduction of competitive tendering.

The LSC's interpretation of Carter reveals a very half-hearted faith in market forces. In the Law Society's response to the BVT consultation, it noted that the LSC's 'advocacy of market rates' was 'conditional on the market holding rates down below certain levels', since if the market rate were to exceed current expenditure the LSC, instead of asking for more money, would control costs by cutting scope. The Law Society concluded that BVT is 'not an appropriate method for procuring defence services'. It argues that the introduction of fee schemes (police station fixed fees and Crown Court graduated litigators' fee and the old standard fees in the magistrates' court) plus VHCC contracting should provide high levels of cost predictability.

Further reform on its way?

At the time of going to press, LAG is keeping a watching brief on two distinct areas of criminal legal aid policy.

A damning report in 2008 by the legal academics Professors Lee Bridges and Ed Cape argued that CDS Direct was of 'questionable legality' under domestic law and possibly in contravention of the European Convention on Human Rights.[27] They argued that the universal right of all suspects to consult a solicitor of their choice has been 'undermined' by the introduction of the helpline. The service was piloted in October 2005 and went national in April 2008. Calls are routed through the Defence Solicitor Call Centre.

The academics accused the ministers of 'suffering from a collective amnesia regarding the lessons of history' which led to the right to consult a lawyer privately and have their presence in police interviews. Under Police and Criminal Evidence Act 1984 s58, any person under arrest and held in custody in a police station or other premises is entitled on request to 'consult a solicitor privately at any time'.

Before CDS Direct, when a person was arrested and detained at a police station and requested a lawyer, the police were obliged to contact that lawyer as soon as possible. According to the academics, now 'even in a straightforward drink-driving case where the suspect is willing to pay privately, they will have to go through six stages of referral before they can speak to their lawyer'. 'More worrying is the fact that this can also be the case for a suspect who is mentally ill,' they argue. 'The schemes may save a small proportion of the legal aid budget, but at what cost to access to justice?' The report claimed that the 'barely veiled underlying intent' of the reforms was 'to place a cap on any further expansion in the take-up of the right to custodial legal advice'.

According to the LSC, CDS Direct saves the taxpayer around £8 million a year. It handled approximately 11,800 cases a month in 2008 and the vast majority (98 per cent) of requests for advice were responded to within 15 minutes. The LSC supplied LAG with a 'random' selection of nine files which were judged by experienced defence lawyers to be of an impressively high quality. LAG has concerns about an increasing reliance on telephone advice, especially at police stations, and will monitor the development of CDS Direct.

LAG is alarmed at plans for making defendants meet the costs of their own defence. The Ministry of Justice published two consultation papers at the end of 2008 on means testing of legal aid in the Crown Court (together with the LSC)[28] and on the awards of costs in criminal cases.[29]

Under the new proposals there will be a pilot covering five Crown Court areas whereby those defendants who fail a new means assessment and are found guilty will have to reimburse the taxpayer for the cost of their defence. The Ministry of Justice is also consulting on possible reforms to the system of payment of acquitted defendants' legal costs. The first option would mean that individuals failing to apply for legal aid in Crown Court cases, who instruct lawyers privately, would no longer be eligible for their legal costs from central funds if acquitted. The second option is to cap payments in all cases for acquitted defendants, including companies, to the relevant legal aid rates. According to the government, the options are 'not mutually exclusive'.

Both the Law Society and Bar Council support 'in principle' the notion that people who can afford to contribute to the cost of their defence should do so. LAG is not convinced that such a system could operate without risking justice. Defendants are involuntary players in the criminal justice system facing the might of the state.

On defence costs, the LSC claimed to be looking at whether it was 'counterintuitive' to pay for higher privately funded rates in cases when lawyers were 'happy' to do the work on legal aid rates. 'Given the number of contracted providers offering criminal legal aid services and the relatively small proportion of privately-funded work available, there is no obvious reason why practitioners should not offer private clients legal aid rates', it said. It went on to say that whilst 'some individuals or companies may in future be willing to pay a premium' to a particular firm, that was 'a financial choice that should not necessarily be subsidised by the taxpayer'. It cannot be right that someone who has been wrongly prosecuted should be left paying the costs of their defence.

1   Lord Irvine of Lairg, speech to Law Society's annual conference, 18 October 1997.
2   *Law Society Gazette* 4 February 1998.
3   Lord Chancellor's Department, *Modernising justice* Cm 4155, TSO, 1998.
4   Consultation paper, *The future of publicly funded legal services*, Law Society, February 2003.
5   Jack Straw, speech to annual police superintendents' conference 14 September 1999.
6   Lee Bridges and Avrom Sherr, *Evaluation of the Public Defender Service in England and Wales*, LSC, 2007.
7   *Independent Lawyer* December/January 2007.
8   *Law Society Gazette* 30 May 2003.
9   Consultation paper, *Delivering value for money in the Criminal Defence Service*, Department for Constitutional Affairs, June 2003.
10 *Law Society Gazette* 20 June 2003.
11 Home Office research study 168, *Managing courts effectively: the reasons for adjournments in magistrates' courts*, 1997.
12 *Route to justice: improving the pathway of offenders through the criminal justice system*, Audit Commission, June 2002.
13 Ed Cape and Richard Moorhead, *Demand induced supply? Identifying cost drivers in criminal defence work*, Legal Services Research Centre, July 2007.
14 House of Commons Home Affairs Committee, *Police funding, fourth report of session 2006–07* HC 553, TSO, 2007.
15 *Independent Lawyer* June 2007.
16 *Daily Telegraph* 29 April 2004.
17 *A fairer deal for legal aid* Cm 6591, TSO, 2005.
18 *Daily Telegraph* 24 July 2005.
19 Lord Carter's review of legal aid procurement, *Procurement of criminal defence services: market-based reform*, February 2006.
20 *Independent Lawyer* June 2007.

21 *Independent Lawyer* March 2006.

22 *Times* 14 February 2006.

23 *Legal aid reform: the way ahead* Cm 6993, TSO, November 2006.

24 Consultation paper, *Legal aid: a sustainable future – analysis of responses*, DCA and LSC, November 2006, para 1.3.

25 *Best value tendering of criminal defence services: a consultation paper*, LSC, December 2007.

26 Roger Smith, *Legal aid contracting*, LAG, 1998, p6.

27 Lee Bridges and Ed Cape, *CDS Direct: flying in the face of the evidence*, Centre for Crime and Justice Studies at King's College London, 2008.

28 Consultation paper CP27/08, *Crown Court means testing*, 6 November 2008.

29 Consultation paper CP28/08, *The award of costs from central funds in criminal cases*, 6 November 2008.

CHAPTER 9

Bridging the gap: proposals and possible solutions

At no point in legal aid's 60-year history has the reality of the publicly funded legal sector ever matched the aspirations laid down in the Rushcliffe report. It has never been a universal service available to all who needed it, a legal services equivalent of the National Health Service.

As this book documents, from the outset the scheme failed to live up to that post-war welfare state vision. In its first incarnation, it was largely restricted to advice and representation for impecunious divorcing spouses and defendants. Between 1973 and 1986 there was growth, spending on legal aid increased, and the scheme covered most civil and criminal problems. This ended in March 1986 when budget constraints meant the government decided to limit scope and eligibility. When the New Labour period began with a new vision to create a 'comprehensive' Community Legal Service (CLS), not only did the government fail to deliver on that manifesto commitment but, in its latter period, legal aid eligibility has shrunk alarmingly making the scheme an irrelevance to most people.

Reports of legal aid's death, to paraphrase Mark Twain, have been much exaggerated. That said, it is LAG's contention that the precarious state of health of the civil scheme means its future is far from certain. Legal aid policy has lost the plot. That is not the fault of the Legal Services Commission (LSC) which have been left the impossible brief of 'reforming' a service according to Lord Carter's blueprint which is already over-stretched and under-funded.

There is an absence of vision for today's CLS and no agreed common principles to provide a secure foundation. At present there is an acute danger that what remains of civil legal aid faces death by a thousand cuts.

This final chapter comprises LAG's proposals and possible solutions to create a legal aid system fit for the 21st century.

LAG's proposals

GENERAL

(1) Call on policy-makers to sign up to the six legal aid foundation principles
(2) Separate the civil and criminal budgets
(3) Establish a means of setting fees which is sustainable for providers and gives a quality service to the public
(4) Reform the Legal Services Commission
(5) Establish the principle of 'polluter pays'
(6) Connect to the communities it serves

CIVIL

(7) Establish a free legal aid service for all
(8) End the social welfare law postcode lottery
(9) Reform the tendering process for local legal services
(10) Promote direct commissioning of specialist services
(11) Research the viability of insurance as a way of providing access to justice
(12) Formalise funding arrangements to supplement the legal aid budget
(13) Consult on establishing a separate social welfare legal aid fund

FAMILY

(14) Ensure there is no impediment to childcare proceedings
(15) Establish a network of coverage in every local area for domestic violence cases

PERSONAL INJURY

(16) Review the operation of conditional fee agreements
(17) Evaluate a contingent legal aid fund

CRIMINAL

(18) Compensate the legal aid budget for external cost drivers
(19) Abandon plans for best value tendering
(20) Reassert the principle that defendants should not have to pay the costs of being wrongly prosecuted

General

(1) Call on policy-makers to sign up to the six legal aid foundation principles

The mismatch between the grand vision of a universal legal service and the reality of relatively well-resourced but shrinking islands of family and criminal legal aid advice floating in an ocean of unmet legal demand is stark. There is an urgent need for a frank cross-party debate about what we as a society expect from legal aid.

Sir Geoffrey Bindman, a legal aid lawyer for nearly 50 years, believes that the legal aid system 'needs to be re-thought from the starting point that equal access to justice is a fundamental principle without which no system of justice is tolerable'. We would hope that this is a concept behind which all political parties could line up.

However, what it means in practice is less than clear. There is a view that the government must be prepared to spend whatever it takes to provide equal access to justice. Unsurprisingly, it is shared by LAG and many of the professionals who work with the growing section of society for whom this is by no means guaranteed. LAG reluctantly acknowledges the improbability of any government expanding the system significantly in the near future.

Unlike health and education budgets, legal aid is set to be cut back in real terms over the next two years. The health budget is set to grow at 4 per cent a year in real terms to £110 billion by 2010/11 and the education budget will grow at a rate of 2.8 per cent in real terms to a total of £74.4 billion. Legal aid, ever the poor relation, will be expected to remain at the level of £2 billion. The current justice minister and Lord Chancellor, Jack Straw, seems resolved to ignore calls for increasing public spending in this area. In a speech to a Labour party conference in 2008, Straw contrasted the UK legal aid budget with other countries. Far from expanding the scheme, Straw provocatively called on the lawyers 'to work with me to find out why our spending is so much greater than other countries – and how we can reduce it'.

Events, of course, can change even a government's best-laid spending plans. At the time of writing, the UK and all western governments are intervening to prop up their banks in the midst of a credit crisis. It seems that the world is entering into a period of greater state intervention in reaction to the problems caused by the deregulated free market. The inevitable consequence of an economic downturn is that more people become entitled to legal aid as they lose jobs and struggle to pay rising bills. So they are going to need help with all the housing, debt, benefit and employment problems that follow. Will a Labour government leave its supporters (as they lose their jobs and their homes) without legal redress? At the very least the economic downturn is likely to force ministers to confront the self-inflicted problem at the heart of the legal aid system: how to reconcile increasing expenditure on criminal legal aid with increasing demand for civil law services within a fixed budget? LAG calls for that debate to be aired as a matter of urgency but within the context of agreeing the principles on which the system is founded. In the introduction, LAG proposed the six foundation principles:

(1) Access to justice is the constitutional right of each citizen
Legal aid was meant to ensure this. The Rushcliffe report, which was the basis on which the modern legal aid system was founded, stated that legal aid should be available in those types of cases in which lawyers normally represented private individual clients. Legal aid should not be limited to those people 'normally classed as poor, but should include those of 'small or moderate means'. The legal aid system never fully realised these ideals. Currently civil legal aid is in danger of becoming a sink service for a minority of the population.

(2) The right to access justice applies equally to civil and criminal law
Civil legal aid, particularly social welfare law, has always been the poor relation in the system. The civil legal aid budget urgently needs to be separated from the growing criminal budget.

(3) The interests of the citizen should determine policy on access to justice issues, not those of the providers of services
Up until 1988 the Law Society administered legal aid. It ran the system largely in the interests of lawyers as opposed to the public. Legal aid policy is still mainly determined by interests groups and not the users of legally aided advice services. The public are not consulted over the type of system they want.

(4) The constitutional right to be regarded as innocent until proved guilty should be respected as a cardinal principle of criminal law

Legal aid was first established at the beginning of the last century for criminal cases as it was increasingly recognised legal representation was essential to guarantee a fair trial. Criminal legal aid is under pressure due to the numerous changes in the law and the administration of justice, but the government fails to recognise this. Equally the inadequacy of some publicly funded services is undermining the protections defendants' rights under legislation such as the Police and Criminal Evidence Act 1984 and the Human Rights Act 1998.

(5) Promoting access to justice requires policies across a range of areas including law reform, education and legal services

The legal aid system has become too focused on funding individual cases. It has neglected its role in wider legal education and the more creative use of the law to tackle legal problems systematically.

(6) Proposals for reform must take account of the realistic levels of resources but these should not be seen as defining policy

The modern legal aid system has been designed on the basis of the legal services that can be bought within the current budget of £2 billion rather than an understanding of who should be under the scheme and to what assistance they should be entitled.

(2) Separate the civil and criminal budgets

The civil legal aid budget must be ring-fenced to protect it from the pressures of expenditure on criminal defence work. At the moment a person's 'right' to access to justice under the civil scheme is conditional on the availability of funds left over from the criminal budget. Or, as the then Lord Chancellor, Lord Irvine put it in a debate on the Access to Justice Bill: 'What is available for civil legal aid is what is left over from the budget after the prior claims of criminal legal aid have been met.'[1] LAG argues that access to justice is a constitutional right for civil and criminal advice without any condition. The legal aid system should reflect that principle in its structure.

(3) Establish a fair means of setting fees

A forum needs to be established to consult with providers on fee levels which leads to fees being set that guarantee good quality services to clients. A review of the numbers of exceptional cases under fixed fees needs to undertaken as a matter of urgency to decide whether suppliers have reduced their numbers of complex cases in order to undertake simple cases within the fixed fee limit.

(4) Reform the Legal Services Commission

The principal reasons for such a body exist today as they did when the Legal Services Commission (LSC) was first proposed. First, the LSC provides decisions on entitlement to legal aid which are independent from the government. Secondly, the shift away from the court-based system of legal aid in criminal cases and the 20 years of experience of administering civil legal aid have built up administrative expertise in a dedicated agency. For these reasons it would be a mistake to contemplate breaking up the LSC.

LAG is concerned, though, that the cutbacks in the LSC's budget mean that this expertise could be lost. The LSC has dropped its plans for the introduction of a preferred supplier scheme and has currently set the level for entering the legal aid contracting system at 'threshold competence'. This indicates a watering down of quality standards. LAG fears that with shrinking resources unless the LSC hands over the control of quality, standards will fall further with the introduction of fixed fees.

LAG proposes that quality control passes to the Legal Services Board (LSB) which currently regulates the legal professions and oversees complaints. The LSB could choose to delegate quality control to the professional bodies while maintaining overarching control. This could lead to the Lexcel quality mark which has been developed by the Law Society replacing the LSC's Specialist Quality Mark. At the time of writing, discussions are ongoing between the LSC, the legal professions and the not-for-profit sector to do this. LAG argues that this might well work but there should be overall control by the LSB.

LAG's main concern about the LSC is its overall strategic direction. The shift to a 'procurement agency' has meant that it has absolved itself of a wider responsibility for promoting 'access to justice', has watered down its role in initiating policy around legal services and largely become a service delivery agency for the Ministry of Justice. This is the main reason why LAG is proposing that policy, research and consultation over legal services are undertaken by other agencies. Legal aid needs a strong non-government advocate, a role for which the LSC is no longer suited.

Finally, LAG calls for 'legal aid' to be reinstated to the official lexicon – at present, the official terminology is 'CLS funding'. Also the 'Community Legal Service' has failed to lodge itself in the public consciousness as a brand. This has been a disappointment (although LAG is reluctant to advocate more expensive re-branding of the Commission). Our preference is for, where possible, the term 'legal aid' to be adopted to describe the public face of the service.

(5) Establish the principle of 'polluter pays'

LAG believes that where possible funds to supplement legal aid should be raised as compensation from parties that contribute to legal problems. Currently the government is supporting the banks due to the financial crisis sparked by their reckless lending and investment policies. LAG believes that banks and other lenders should pay for debt counselling services as part of their corporate social responsibility policies. Due to the recent large-scale state intervention in the banking sector the government is in a stronger position to make the case. We would suggest that the ratio of funding between the state and lenders should be reversed so that the lenders pay the bulk of the costs of dealing with debt problems. Hopefully this could be achieved on a voluntary basis, if not a compulsory levy could be introduced.

The Legal Services Act 2007 already allows for costs in pro bono cases to be paid into a central fund administered by the Access to Justice Foundation. The foundation is also developing regional organisations. A voluntary or compulsory levy on lenders could be paid into the same or another charitable fund, along with compensation awards made in class actions with a public interest element. For example, a drugs company found to be negligent could be required to pay a sum in as part of a compensation award.

(6) Connect legal aid to the communities it serves

The legal aid scheme has so far failed to engage meaningfully with the communities which it seeks to serve. There is well-documented concern about gaps in the provision of legally aided advice and a failure in the signposting of such services locally. The precarious funding arrangements of the not-for-profit sector, the rolling experiment that is the introduction of fixed fees, as well as the reliance on telephone services mean that 'access to justice' on the ground is a fluid notion.

The degree to which the LSC can be an effective 'commissioner' of publicly-funded legal services is compromised by a lack of funding and a strategic retrenching to a London-based commissioning body with little presence in the regions. The failure of the LSC to engage with communities (through the aborted £4 million CLS partnerships initiative and now the present difficulties with joint commissioning through community legal advice centres) does not mean that it is not worth pursuing. The ability to do so is essential.

For all concerned with legal aid, a continuing priority must be how best to co-ordinate the provision of legal aid services so that they are accessible to all.

LAG proposes that the research and planning resources from the LSC are transferred to an external body such as the Civil Justice Council (CJC) and an agency to undertake work around criminal legal aid. These organisations could co-ordinate consultation with the public and research the availability of advice. LAG, and other charities not representing practitioner interests, could ensure users are party to this process. The CJC would enable the users of legal aid to have a say in how the services are designed and monitor the availability of advice. Family legal aid could be planned through the CJC or else the Family Justice Councils. There is currently a network of 39 of these co-ordinating family law services under a national board.

The 42 local Criminal Justice Boards under their national body, which have been established to co-ordinate criminal justice services at a local level, could be given a role in planning legal aid provided that this did not create a conflict of interest with the courts and police being participants in this forum.

Civil

(7) Establish a free legal aid service for all

LAG calls for a free service for all to provide basic information and advice on civil law. We propose a national telephone advice service supported by comprehensive legal materials available online and in print form in order to improve public legal education on rights.

The bones of such a service already exist through Citizens Advice's fledgling telephone advice line and online advice guide and the LSC's Community Legal Advice (formally Community Legal Service Direct). The new Legal Aid Direct would not have a means test but would be open to every UK resident.

It perhaps is unavoidable to have to consider the future of legal help in this country: what it pays for and how effective it is in resolving clients' problems.

There is also the possibility of using resources from the private sector to partially fund the service by paying fees for referrals for personal injury cases. An agreement could also be reached with the insurance industry to provide some of the service, subject to controls over the quality, in return for the income from referral fees.

A second aim of the telephone service would be to work on systemic issues in a similar way to that in which Citizens Advice, law centres and other not-for-profit agencies attempt to do at the moment. Information through telephone and internet contacts could be collated to feed back into this work, providing evidence of the effectiveness of government policy and administration. For example, numbers of telephone calls could increase over problems to do with claiming a particular benefit and this could be used as evidence to change the way in which it is administered.

(8) End the social welfare law postcode lottery

Social welfare law has always been the poor relation in the civil legal aid system, while family and criminal take up the bulk of the budget. As the table at page 68 clearly illustrates there is a massive disparity in provision of such services. It is a postcode lottery for clients faced with employment, debt, housing, immigration and public law problems. The availability of services has been affected by the reforms of legal aid described in Chapters 3 and 4. The numbers of social welfare law providers has declined as firms have left the system through a combination of market forces and an unwillingness to engage with the bureaucracy of legal aid. The table in Appendix C illustrates this sharp decline, for example the number of housing law providers has fallen from 799 in 2000/01 to 362 in September 2007.

Unless client services are matched with other resources, often from local government funding, clients only receive a partial service particularly in those areas of law such as benefits and employment in which tribunal representation is out of scope. Again the level of service they receive is dependent on whether they are lucky enough to live in an area in which services are funded to provide representation.

A comprehensive Telephone Advice Service would increase resources for work currently out of scope.

(9) Reform the tendering process for local legal services

LAG agrees that, as far as possible, services should work closely together at a local level to deal with the clusters of interrelated problems often faced by clients. We have, though, consistently opposed the LSC plans for joint tenders with local authorities. We believe these tenders are too rigid as they foist monopolies on local areas, taking no consideration of existing services such as citizens' advice bureaux and the other resources they have such as volunteers and charitable funding. Local authorities are also extremely reluctant to deal with the LSC and this reticence means that many such endeavours inevitably wither away.

LAG would suggest a return to the contracting approach to procuring local services, though the option to tender could be retained if some local authorities preferred to work in this way. The community legal services grant system would be used to fill the gaps in the system identified by the research done by the Criminal Justice Centre (CJC) or others. Such a body's aim will be to monitor the availability of civil legal services across the country to ensure a fairer distribution of services.

(10) Encourage direct commissioning of specialist services

LAG is not proposing to expand generalist advice at the expense of specialist advice. It shares concerns that the current system is 'dumbing down' by reducing the availability of specialist services as providers seek to increase the throughput of simple cases to compensate for the loss in income caused by fixed fees. A helpline service could be effective in dealing with many problems over the phone, freeing the network of specialist providers to undertake detailed casework. There needs to be a fund allocated within the overall budget for legal aid to develop specialist civil law services to fill the gaps identified by the CJC and to supplement the already established network of specialist providers.

The proposed fund would provide grants to develop services in areas with inadequate coverage. It would look to provide joined-up services along similar lines to the current community legal advice centres model. Local councils would be offered a community legal services grant to establish the new services or reconfigure existing services to provide coverage across the five areas of social welfare law. There would be no compulsion to tender for the services, if local councils could choose either to establish these services through not-for-profit agencies with community governance or to run open tenders. Priorities for such services would be set with reference to relieving social exclusion and public policy needs, rather than just dealing with cases within scope and eligibility. For example, housing, debt, domestic violence or discrimination cases could receive help regardless of whether the clients passed a means test.

(11) Research the viability of legal expenses insurance as a way of providing access to justice

LAG calls for another look at the potential for legal expenses insurance to provide access to justice. While such insurance policies are of limited use in their present form, the continental European experience suggests that legal expenses insurance could play a greater part in providing access to justice.

Just under half of the adult population in the UK is covered by legal expenses insurance, usually purchased as an 'add-on' with their home or motor insurance. Many people also have insurance through membership of a trade union or other organisation. It is reckoned that in Germany some 45 per cent of the population is covered by legal expenses insurance. There are cultural differences. In Germany the idea of protecting yourself against risk is firmly entrenched in the national psyche. One critical distinction is Germans buy legal expenses insurance as a standalone product. In other words they buy it because they want it (as opposed to the UK where it is often included as an 'add on' when policy buyers buy other kinds of insurance). In Germany and elsewhere on the continent, the policy covers almost all risk types for all the main legal problems, and some products even include divorce (although subject to restrictions). In the UK policy holders are often not aware of the existence of the cover or, if they are, of what it might cover (which in turn keeps premiums down).

Promotion of legal expenses insurance (and the availability of competitively priced standalone products) could enable a section of the population who can afford insurance but not the services of private practice lawyers to have access to justice.

LAG calls for the government to encourage the greater take-up of legal expenses insurance in partnership with the insurance industry and a rebranding to raise consumer awareness ('private legal aid', perhaps). If legal expenses insurance is to be a significant component in enabling people to have legal redress, it could be integrated with the publicly-funded legal advice sector. So, for example, insurer-funded helplines could link with the new telephone helpline service which would field all calls, provide generalist help and then refer callers on for further specialist advice through the publicly-funded sector, their union or insurer. However, LAG would be keen to prevent the development of a two-tier service with those clients not holding 'private legal aid' insurance being excluded from the system.

A major advantage of before-the-event insurance in personal injury cases is that it reduces claims' costs as there are no success fees and, if it works correctly, cases with a chance of success of 50 per cent or higher should be backed, in contrast to conditional fee arrangements which usually require a much higher chance of success. LAG is, however, concerned about the payment of referral fees and the lack of transparency of arrangements whereby solicitors buy work from insurers and then take cases on conditional fee agreements. It seems iniquitous that insurers should profit twice – from insurance premiums and then referral fees – in what are effectively 'win-win' deals. If transparency around such policies can be achieved, then some of those funds should be directed back into assisting accident victims, perhaps, through the proposed telephone service.

(12) Formalise funding arrangements to supplement the legal aid budget

In Chapter 2 we described the parallel legal aid service which has evolved in the voluntary sector. This is the largest part of non-legal aid funded work and yet the variable commitment of local authority funding means that such a vital service is built on the shakiest of foundations. As LAG has said before, local authorities should be under a statutory duty to provide an adequate service and the cost should be recognised as essential by central government.

(13) Consult on establishing a separate social welfare legal aid fund

A separate social welfare law fund could be established to be administered by a charitable or other organisation independent of government. The organisation could distribute legal aid funding for social welfare law as well as the grant scheme described above. It could also raise funding from other sources. For example, it could combine or work in tandem with the Access to Justice Foundation to raise funds from pro bono cases, distribute funds raised from the financial services sector and seek to raise funds from the private legal sector through donations from interest on clients' accounts and other sources.

Family

(14) Ensure there is no impediment to childcare proceedings

LAG is alarmed about the consequences of government policy to make courts self-financing and, in particular, its likely impact on deterring local authorities from bringing childcare proceedings. In 2008 such court fees went up from £150 to £4,000 and £4,825 if a case goes to a full hearing. It is concerned that the combined impact of such a huge fee increase and new court procedures is acting as a deterrent which led within months of their implementation to a marked drop in child care and supervision orders.

The idea behind the fee change was to recover the £35 million costs to the court system. Ministers claim that they are increasing funding to compensate for the fee change, however LAG is concerned that such money is not ring-fenced for care cases. LAG does not accept the suggested rationale for making the courts self-financing, not least when the welfare of vulnerable children is at stake.

(15) Establish a network of coverage for domestic violence cases

As discussed in Chapter 6, LAG is concerned about the lack of coverage of specialist solicitors in domestic violence cases. We suggest a grant scheme could also be used to cover these gaps, where possible including these services with social welfare law providers.

Personal injury

(16) Review the operation of conditional fee agreements

There is a real need for scrutiny of the working of conditional fee agreements to establish whether consumers are treated fairly in accident claims. It seems that the more severe problems that bedevilled Conditional Fee Arrangements (CFAs) in the early days – mainly, accident victims' damages being swallowed by legal and other costs and 'hard sell' tactics by claims companies – have been addressed through the courts and through the belated introduction of regulation. LAG calls for rigorous research into the client impact of 'no win, no fee' for accident claims, as well as the operation contingency fees in employment tribunals.

Outside of mainstream personal injury, there is considerable doubt about access to justice, especially in complex group actions and litigations where after-the-event insurance is either unavailable or not affordable.

(17) Evaluate a contingent legal aid fund

A contingent legal aid fund could become the poor relation of 'no win, no fee' (conditional fee) arrangements, but there is an argument to say that such a fund could be established for class actions. The LSC would provide the initial finance to underwrite the fund and it could eventually become self-financing.

Criminal

(18) Compensate the legal aid budget for external cost drivers

A significant proportion of the increase in expenditure in the criminal legal aid budget over the last decade has been a direct consequence of decisions beyond the control of the legal aid system. The government needs to understand properly those external factors that drive up the budget. So, for example, it must acknowledge that the greater use of law enforcement from arrest to imprisonment leads to more expenditure on criminal legal aid. Since coming to power the Labour government has increased expenditure on policing by 40 per cent in real terms, boosting the number of police officers by 14,233, as well as introducing some 60 pieces of criminal justice legislation. In a ring-fenced budget the government would not have the option of raiding the civil budget for funds.

(19) Abandon plans for best value tendering

Under the Rushcliffe principles the purpose of the legal aid system is to provide access to justice for majority of the population. Criminal legal aid largely serves this purpose. It provides a service to the vast majority of people if they are accused of a crime.

At the time of going to press, there is considerable unhappiness among defence practitioners, mainly due to reductions in fees. However there is little evidence of gaps in coverage across the country for police station and magistrates' court work. This government needs to tread very carefully and to take seriously concerns about alienating the defence profession.

Costs in magistrates' court and police station work are under control and LAG sees little merit in the proposal to introduced best value tendering for this work.

(20) Reassert the principle that defendants should not have to pay the costs of being wrongly prosecuted

At the time of going to press the government was consulting on a change in the law that would end a century-old right for cleared defendants to have their legal costs reimbursed. The right was enshrined in statute, culminating in the Prosecution of Offences Act 1985. The Ministry of Justice published two consultation papers towards the end of 2008 on means testing of legal aid in the Crown Court (together with the Legal Services Commission)[2] and on the awards of costs in criminal cases.[3]

Ministers are looking at possible reforms to the system of payment of acquitted defendants' legal costs. The first option would mean that individuals failing to apply for legal aid in Crown Court cases, who instruct lawyers privately, would no longer be eligible for their legal costs from central funds if acquitted. The second option would be to cap payments in all cases for acquitted defendants to the relevant legal aid rates.

LAG is concerned about the impact of such reforms. Defendants are involuntary players in the criminal justice system facing the might of the state. Means testing in the Crown Court could risk miscarriages of justice, which is unacceptable. Similarly, if people are not going to recover their costs, more will choose not to instruct lawyers, with equally dismal results.

1   HL Debates col 738, 21 January 1999.
2   Consultation paper CP27/08, *Crown Court means testing*, 6 November 2008.
3   Consultation paper CP28/08, *The award of costs from central funds in criminal cases*, 6 November 2008.

Table showing number of firms and spending on criminal and civil legal aid

	2000–2001	2001–2002	2002–2003	2003–2004	2004–2005	2005–2006	2006–2007
Civil Legal Aid							
number of firms	4,860	4,543	4,641	4,301	3,989	3,632	3,437
total amount spent (£M)	791.9	734.5	812.8	897.9	845.9	831	808.9
Total Case Number ('000s)							
CLS Licensed	275.5	225.4	204.5	215.3	201.9	194.8	179.5
Family Licensed	129.4	141.0	128.8	134.8	133.5	130.6	127.7
Legal Help Work	862.0	779.6	812.9	709.8	654.3	801.4	884.6
Criminal Legal Aid							
number of firms	2,925	2,909	2,900	2,669	2,643	2,608	2,510
total amount spent (£M)	872.4	982.1	1095.7	1178.0	1192.1	1196.8	1171.4
Police Station							
number of cases ('000)	760.5	760.5	753.0	771.7	781.0	770.1	802.2
amount spent (£000)	117.3	140.2	168.8	175.5	172.2	174.3	177.6
Lower Courts							
number of cases ('000)	467.6	623.6	796.6	808.1	724.7	720.1	634.4
amount spent (£M)	232.9	220.5	337.9	340.2	325.0	329.8	309.3
Higher Courts							
number of cases ('000)	116.0	115.0	123.7	124.0	115.6	121.5	120.7
amount spent (£M)	422.0	474.1	569.3	645.0	682.4	695.5	647.9
Not For Profit Legal Aid							
number of organizations	367	389	420	414	441	469	458

Legal Aid gross cash spend by 'social welfare' category, 1997/98 to 2007/08

Category of Law	Community Care[1]			Debt[2]			Employment	
Year Scheme	Completed Matters	Gross Claim Value £'000	Hours Reported	Completed Matters	Gross Claim Value £'000	Hours Reported	Completed Matters	Gross Claim Value £'000
1997/98[4]								
'Green Form' A&A	na	na		87,180	6,947		20,923	2,047
Civil Representation[5]	na	na		na	na		244	na
Totals 1997/98	na	na		87,180	6,947		21,167	2,047
1998/99[4]								
'Green Form' A&A	na	na		83,175	6,822		19,629	2,038
Civil Representation[5]	na	na		na	na		219	na
Totals 1998/99	na	na		83,175	6,822		19,848	2,038
1999/2000[4]								
'Green Form' A&A	na	na		72,066	6,406		17,034	1,936
Solicitor Contracts	386	64		13,475	1,277		3,556	468
NfP Contracts[6]	5	*1*	17	2,638	*1,383*	18,279	361	*255*
Civil Representation[7]	1	1		1,684	5,629		299	1,364
Totals 1999/2000	392	65	17	89,863	14,694	18,279	21,250	4,022
2000/01								
'Green Form' A&A	na	na		3,549	317		799	99
Solicitor Contracts	1,672	324		36,739	3,837		10,324	1,579
NfP Contracts[6]	102	*22*	240	14,204	*8,173*	88,239	2,630	*1,839*
Civil Representation[7]	25	41		1,624	6,415		260	1,506
Totals 2000/01[8]	1,799	388	240	56,116	18,742	88,239	14,013	5,024
2001/02								
'Green Form' A&A	na	na		701	69		181	22
Solicitor Contracts	2,093	546		30,304	3,716		8,674	1,738
NfP Contracts[6]	137	46	586	21,181	*11,298*	142,472	2,731	*1,963*
Housing Court DS Pilot	–	–		–	–		–	–
Civil Representation[7]	162	374		1,059	4,923		173	1,287
Totals 2001/02[8]	2,392	967	586	53,245	20,007	142,472	11,759	5,009

	Housing[3]			Welfare Benefits			All Social Welfare Law		
Hours Reported	Completed Matters	Gross Claim Value £'000	Hours Reported	Completed Matters	Gross Claim Value £'000	Hours Reported	Completed Matters	Gross Claim Value £'000	Hours Reported
	120,252	13,825		189,537	15,762		417,892	38,581	
	15,083	na		na	na		15,327	na	
	135,335	13,825		189,537	15,762		417,892	38,581	
	119,839	14,580		184,613	16,651		407,256	40,091	
	14,876	na		na	na		15,095	na	
	134,715	14,580		184,613	16,651		407,256	40,091	
	106,187	13,262		147,338	14,903		342,625	36,508	
	25,073	3,244		22,965	2,755		65,455	7,806	
3,369	2,262	881	11,645	5,459	2,152	28,457	10,725	4,672	61,767
	12,897	35,501		149	335		15,030	42,829	
3,369	146,419	52,888	11,645	175,911	20,145	28,457	433,835	91,815	61,767
	5,392	654		7,267	719		17,007	1,789	
	75,023	10,500		66,004	8,784		189,762	25,025	
19,855	13,533	5,134	55,427	28,080	12,711	137,228	58,549	27,880	300,989
	12,787	36,714		174	464		14,870	45,141	
19,855	106,735	53,002	55,427	101,525	22,678	137,228	280,188	99,834	300,989
	1,219	162		1,102	130		3,203	384	
	73,255	12,193		51,763	8,034		166,089	26,227	
24,749	18,505	6,828	86,107	34,523	15,410	194,326	77,077	35,546	448,239
	na	194		–	–		–	194	
	11,233	34,042		200	505		12,827	41,132	
24,749	104,212	53,420	86,107	87,588	24,079	194,326	259,196	103,482	448,239

Category of Law	Community Care[1]			Debt[2]			Employment	
Year Scheme	Completed Matters	Gross Claim Value £'000	Hours Reported	Completed Matters	Gross Claim Value £'000	Hours Reported	Completed Matters	Gross Claim Value £'000
2002/03								
'Green Form' A&A	na	na		79	9		25	4
Solicitor Contracts	2,462	776		26,444	3,712		8,717	2,314
NfP Contracts[6]	182	86	1,292	30,595	14,020	210,219	3,729	2,236
Housing Court DS Pilot	–	–		–	–		–	–
Civil Representation[7]	290	1,107		768	4,293		143	966
Totals 2002/03[8]	**2,934**	**1,969**	**1,292**	**57,886**	**22,035**	**210,219**	**12,614**	**5,520**
2003/04								
'Green Form' A&A	na	na		0	0		0	0
Solicitor Contracts	2,911	1,101		20,175	3,056		7,178	2,374
NfP Contracts[6]	214	116	1,685	35,724	14,311	208,759	4,042	2,158
Housing Court DS Pilot	–	–		–	–		–	–
Civil Representation[7]	439	1,505		672	3,852		184	1,183
Totals 2003/04[8]	**3,564**	**2,721**	**1,685**	**56,571**	**21,219**	**208,759**	**11,404**	**5,716**
2004/05								
Solicitor Contracts[9]	2,878	1,056		15,234	2,451		5,436	1,995
NfP Contracts[6]	240	149	1,988	39,658	15,362	204,900	4,315	2,390
CLS Direct/CLA[10]	–	–		10,119	1,625		1,751	281
Housing Court DS Pilot	–	–		–	–		–	–
Civil Representation[7]	490	1,844		567	3,596		106	515
Totals 2004/05[8]	**3,608**	**3,049**	**1,988**	**65,578**	**23,035**	**204,900**	**11,608**	**5,181**
2005/06								
Solicitor Contracts[9]	3,242	1,186		15,734	2,566		5,607	2,022
NfP Contracts[6]	442	241	3,402	49,159	18,205	257,074	4,584	2,330
CLS Direct/CLA[10]	–	–		27,100	1,864		10,512	723
Housing Court DS Pilot	–	–		–	–		–	–
Civil Representation[7]	549	2,332		603	3,021		120	1,204
Totals 2005/06[8]	**4,233**	**3,760**	**3,402**	**92,596**	**25,656**	**257,074**	**20,823**	**6,279**

Hours Reported	Housing[3]			Welfare Benefits			All Social Welfare Law		
	Completed Matters	Gross Claim Value £'000	Hours Reported	Completed Matters	Gross Claim Value £'000	Hours Reported	Completed Matters	Gross Claim Value £'000	Hours Reported
	173	23		203	25		480	62	
	67,176	12,607		40,371	7,000		145,170	26,410	
33,523	23,134	7,389	110,790	45,516	16,675	250,024	103,156	40,406	605,849
	na	870		–	–		–	870	
	12,308	36,239		136	395		13,645	43,000	
33,523	102,791	57,129	110,790	86,226	24,096	250,024	262,451	110,748	605,849
	3	0		0	0		3	0	
	57,949	12,083		32,049	5,768		120,262	24,383	
31,485	26,092	7,309	106,614	47,054	16,200	236,323	113,126	40,094	584,866
	na	608		–	–		–	608	
	13,555	39,508		94	376		14,944	46,424	
31,485	97,599	59,509	106,614	79,197	22,344	236,323	248,335	111,509	584,866
	52,219	11,783		25,597	5,048		101,364	22,333	
31,877	29,188	8,406	112,125	46,942	16,224	216,394	120,343	42,531	567,284
	1,588	255		5,447	875		18,905	3,037	
	na	625		–	–		–	625	
	12,767	38,305		60	230		13,990	44,490	
31,877	95,762	59,374	112,125	78,046	22,376	216,394	254,602	113,016	567,284
	55,888	12,689		23,747	4,836		104,218	23,299	
32,898	36,343	9,970	140,787	55,904	18,097	255,540	146,432	48,843	689,701
	12,460	857		14,209	977		64,281	4,421	
	12,031	1,141		–	–		12,031	1,141	
	13,050	38,145		61	374		14,383	45,076	
32,898	129,772	62,802	140,787	93,921	24,284	255,540	341,345	122,781	689,701

Category of Law	Community Care[1]			Debt[2]			Employment	
Year Scheme	Completed Matters	Gross Claim Value £'000	Hours Reported	Completed Matters	Gross Claim Value £'000	Hours Reported	Completed Matters	Gross Claim Value £'000
2006/07								
Solicitor Contracts[9]	3,702	1,335		16,541	2,668		5,738	1,886
NfP Contracts[6]	450	185	3,171	67,054	19,569	335,939	5,962	2,123
CLS Direct/CLA[10]	–	–		36,144	2,915		7,785	628
Housing Court DS Pilot	–	–		–	–		–	–
Civil Representation[7]	557	2,645		463	2,122		121	587
Totals 2006/07[8]	4,709	4,164	3,171	120,202	27,274	335,939	19,606	5,224
2007/08								
Apr–Sep								
Solicitor Contracts[9]	1,791	647		7,810	1,230		2,297	731
NfP Contracts[6]	325	125	2,476	40,769	9,376	186,133	3,874	1,172
Oct–Mar								
Solicitor Contracts[11]	1,664	562		7,162	1,226		2,072	601
NfP Contracts[11]	345	46		36,971	4,249		3,209	576
CLS Direct/CLA[10]	–	–		18,514	2,685		9,527	1,382
Housing Court DS Pilot	–	–		–	–		–	–
Civil Representation[7]	555	2,908		482	2,321		97	706
Totals 2007/08	4,680	4,289	2,476	111,708	21,088	186,133	21,076	5,169

1 Community Care was not coded as a separate category before January 2000.
2 'Hire Purchase & Debt' until 2000/01.
3 'Landlord & Tenant, Housing' until 2000/01.
4 Excludes Legal Aid Board Block Contracting pilots.
5 Pre-Corporate Information System system generally reported on civil bills by forum and type of action, eg Tort, Negligence, not by subject-matter. Certificate numbers for Employment Appeal Tribunals and Landlord & Tenant included as an indication of volume.
6 NfP claim values estimated by pro-rating Standard Monthly Payments spend to hours claimed.
7 Civil representation claim values based on gross costs in closed cases, including set-off cases.
8 Excludes 'Methods of Delivery' pilots.
9 Contract claim values from 2004/05 onwards are fixed fee values.

Hours Reported	Housing[3]			Welfare Benefits			All Social Welfare Law		
	Completed Matters	Gross Claim Value £'000	Hours Reported	Completed Matters	Gross Claim Value £'000	Hours Reported	Completed Matters	Gross Claim Value £'000	Hours Reported
	56,573	12,336		23,504	4,708		106,058	22,933	
36,454	42,669	9,553	163,995	70,045	17,134	294,147	186,180	48,564	833,706
	28,988	2,338		24,196	1,951		97,113	7,832	
	27,562	2,869		–	–		27,562	2,869	
	12,887	37,704		87	370		14,115	43,427	
36,454	168,679	64,800	163,995	117,832	24,164	294,147	431,028	125,626	833,706
	26,774	5,786		11,285	2,264		49,957	10,659	
23,273	25,063	4,805	95,385	43,740	8,389	166,538	113,771	23,868	473,805
	24,196	4,947		10,631	2,086		45,725	9,423	
	20,057	2,499		39,100	4,223		99,677	11,593	
	20,558	2,981		15,226	2,208		63,825	9,256	
	30,472	3,010		–	–		30,472	3,010	
	12,003	35,825		46	158		13,183	41,919	
23,273	159,118	59,854	95,385	120,028	19,327	166,538	416,610	109,727	473,805

10 Community Legal Service Direct/Community Legal Advice claim values estimated by pro-rating total specialist contract value to completed matters by category.

11 Replacement fixed fees from October 2007, as at 26 August 2008.

Table showing the breakdown of social welfare law contracts by category

Social Welfare Law Contracts								
	2000/01	2001/02	2002/03	2003/04	2004/05	2005/06	2006/07	Sep-07
Debt	502	315	276	219	158	144	134	118
Employment	384	256	218	194	151	151	128	107
Housing	799	673	563	504	450	422	410	362
Asylum*					380	327	239	186
Immigration	458	438	500	521	376	326	236	183
Public Law	5	20	28	36	40	45	44	49
Welfare Benefits	505	347	299	240	186	159	136	116

* included with immigration until 2004/05

Bibliography

Legal Aid by Robert Egerton, (1945) pub by Butler and Tanner Ltd

Legal Aid and Advice – Report of the Law Society and the Comments and Recommendations of the Lord Chancellor's Advisory Committee, (1969–70)

Legal Services in Birmingham, L Bridges, B Sufin, J Whetton and R White, Birmingham University, (1975)

Legal services for the community, Michael Zander (1978), pub by Temple Smith

Community Law Centres: A Critical Appraisal, Mike Stephens, (1990) pub by Avebury

The Search for Justice: An Anatomy of the Law, Rozenberg (1994) pub by Hodder and Sloughton

Barriers to Justice Sept, (1995) pub by NACAB

Shaping the Future: New Directions in Legal Services edited by Roger Smith, (1995) pub by LAG

Justice Redressing the Balance by Roger Smith, (1997) pub by LAG

Legal Aid Contracting, Roger Smith (1998) pub by LAG

Practising Welfare Rights, Neil Batcman, (2000) pub by Routledge

Civil Legal Aid in England and Wales 1914 to 1961 Tamara Goriely (2003). University College London (unpublished thesis)

Causes of Action: Civil Law and Social Justice The Final Report of the First LSRC Survey of Justifiable Problems Pascoe Pleasence et al (2004) pub by TSO

The Future of Publicly Funded Legal Service Law Society, Feb 2003

'A fairer deal for legal aid', July 2005 pub by DCA

Index

BPP Pro Bono Centre

About the centre

BPP Pro Bono Centre based at BPP Law School in Leeds, London and Manchester runs a wide variety of projects to which our students can volunteer their time, legal skills and knowledge to help those who may not otherwise have access to legal services. Student volunteers gain practical legal experience and an understanding of the role of law in society while providing important services to the community under the supervision of volunteer BPP lecturers and practitioners.

The centre's projects have won several awards, including The Lawyer's award for pro bono activity of the year 2005 and finalist status for the same award in both 2004 and 2007, plus two high commendations in the Attorney General's student and law school pro bono awards 2007.

Our philosophy

We recognise the inequality and injustice inherent in our society's unmet legal needs and strive to enhance access to justice by promoting and facilitating the provision of pro bono legal services.

Our goals

- To provide our students with the opportunity to participate in pro bono work that matches their interests and level of commitment

- To help the local and broader community by offering a pro bono legal service

- To express our students' and staff's commitment to the pro bono ethic

- To contribute to the legal profession in the UK and abroad by researching and publicising pro bono initiatives

Our activities and projects

Activities and projects are diverse and include:

- **BPP Legal Advice Clinic** - Student advisers work together with legal advisers (volunteer barristers and solicitors) to provide members of the public with initial advice over the telephone on employment law issues

- **Human Rights Unit** - Our students provide supporting legal research to organisations such as Amicus, Amnesty International, Interights, the Solicitors' International Human Rights Group, the European Human Rights Advocacy Centre, Reprieve and the International Bar Association's Human Rights Institute

- **Streetlaw** - Our students provide interactive learning presentations on the law to various groups including primary and secondary school pupils, prison inmates, community groups and the homeless

LAW SCHOOL
preparing you for practice

LAG membership scheme

We welcome membership from all individuals or organisations that share or wish to support our aims and objectives (see www.lag.org.uk/objectives).

Individual members receive:

■ Members' updates via e-mail with policy reports.

■ Invitations to the AGM and other select LAG events.

■ Opportunities to contribute to LAG's campaigns through e-mail and to our online surveys.

■ 10% reduction in the price of LAG training courses, *Legal Action* and *Community Care Law* Reports subscriptions and all our publications ordered directly from us.

Business and organisation members receive all the benefits of individual membership as well as:

■ Two complimentary annual subscriptions to Legal Action.

■ Opportunities to underwrite LAG programmes, events and/or campaigns, either financially or in kind.

www.lag.org.uk/membership